ONLY GOD

ONLY GOD

Overcoming Trials and Tribulations
With The Power of God and His Word

Jim and Carolyn Barber

authorHOUSE®

AuthorHouse™
1663 Liberty Drive
Bloomington, IN 47403
www.authorhouse.com
Phone: 1-800-839-8640

Published by AuthorHouse   05/16/2013

ISBN: 978-1-4817-5330-2 (sc)
ISBN: 978-1-4817-5329-6 (e)

Contents

Eagle In A Storm

Did you know that an eagle knows, long before a storm starts when one is approaching? The eagle will fly to some high spot and wait for the winds to come. When the storm hits, the eagle sets its wings, so that the wind will pick it up and lift it above the storm. While the storm rages below, the eagle is soaring above it.

The eagle doesn't escape the storm. It simply uses the storm to lift it higher. It rises on the winds, which bring the storm. When the storms of life come upon us, we can rise above them by setting our minds and our beliefs toward God. The storms do not have to overcome us, but rather we can allow God's power to lift us above them.

God enables us to ride the winds of the storm that bring sickness, tragedy, failure and disappointment in our lives, so we can soar above the storm. Remember it is not the burdens of life, that weigh us down; it is how we handle them.

But they that wait upon the Lord shall renew their strength. They shall mount up with wings like eagles; they shall run and not be weary; they shall walk and not faint.—Isaiah 40:31-

Dedication To Jesus

Jesus Christ is the beloved Son of God.

He is despised and rejected of men, a man of sorrows and acquainted with grief: and we hid as it were our faces from Him; He was despised and we esteemed Him not. Surely He hath borne our grief and carried our sorrows; yet we did esteem Him stricken, smitten of God, and afflicted. But He was wounded for our transgressions, He was bruised for our iniquities; the chastisement of our peace was upon Him & with His stripes we were healed. ~Isaiah 53:3-5~

Jesus Christ is God's only begotten Son, yet He came from the throne of His Father to the womb of a woman. He became the Son of man so that we might become sons of God.

He was conceived by the Holy Spirit, and born of a virgin. He lived in poverty, and was unknown outside of Nazareth. He had neither wealth nor influence.

He laid aside His purple robe for a peasant's gown. He was rich, yet for our sakes He became poor. He slept in another man's stable; He rode another man's donkey; He was buried in another man's grave.

History has never known such as He. In infancy, He startled a king. As a boy, He stunned the theologians with His knowledge and wisdom, for His knowledge was directly from God.

In manhood, He ruled the elements and quieted the raging sea. He healed without medicine, and fed thousands from a boy's lunch. Even demons obeyed Him and He gave back life to those who were dead.

He suffered and sustained in body and soul the anger of God against the sin of the whole human race. He was despised and rejected of men. Though He was innocent, He was condemned by a civil judge and sentenced to death on a cross.

By His suffering, death and resurrection, He paid completely for the sins of all who believe in Him. He set us free from the certain judgment and eternal condemnation of God that was to fall on all of us.

Some have given their lives for others, and great men have come and gone, yet Jesus Christ lives on. Herod could not kill Him. Satan could not stop him. Death could not destroy Him. The grave could not hold Him. Having fully satisfied God's perfect justice, He conquered death, hell and the grave and rose on the third day as He said He would.

For the last 2,000 years, every man, woman and child has been confronted with this same question. In Mathew 16:15, Jesus put it this way, "But who do you say that I am" One of His disciples, Simon Peter, replied: "You are the Christ, the Son of the living God." Now it's your turn. Who do you say that He is?

Lord Jesus Christ, take our freedom, our memory, our understanding, and our will. All that we have and cherish, You have given us. We surrender it all to be guided by Your will. Your love and Your grace are wealth enough for us. Give us these, Lord Jesus, and we ask for nothing more. Amen.

Stir up the fire of your faith! Jesus Christ is not a figure of the past. He is not a memory lost in history. He lives! As Paul says, "Jesus Christ is the same yesterday, today and forever."

OUR FAMILY
Seburn and Stacy Puckett: our daughter and her
husband
Cody Oren Tatum and Cameron Marshall Puckett, our
two grandsons

Introduction

We need to wake up to the fact that we are in Spiritual Warfare and it is definitely getting worse every day! It is an all out war against the children of God and what they stand for. Truthfully, we are in a lifetime struggle with the devil and our eternal destiny is at stake. We look around to see Jesus being taken out of the schools, the courtroom and now they are trying to take Christian broadcasting off the air. The saddest thing is, that in some churches, songs about Jesus' precious blood are being taken out of the songbook. There, seemingly is no appreciation for the shedding of Jesus' precious blood for us.

If you are not presently engaged in a spiritual warfare with the enemy (the devil), it is a fact you will be sooner or later. When we make a stand for God we will be faced with many trials and tribulations. There are a lot of people, who are falling by the wayside, because they are not rooted in God and His Word. In some cases, people blame God for what is happening to them. Sometimes, even the strongest Christian, in the midst of their toughest trial, will throw their hands up and walk away.

We have seen this happen to many times. God's children need to realize, that their trials may not only last for just a short time, but also indeed in some cases (like ours), they can continue for months or even years. Our trials are to help us grow and trust in God, like we never have before. They come into our lives, not to tear us down, but to build us up in God.

Dear Friend, you are precious to God. No matter how you treated God in the past, He has never given up on you. God knows all your secrets, your hidden fears and your desperate needs and even your innermost thoughts. No matter who you are, where you are or what you have done, He loves you and He wants the best for you.

God's love for you is a gift—freely given and not something that you have earned. He made it available to every person—red, yellow, black or white, man or woman and its not cheap. God's own precious Son, Jesus Christ has purchased your freedom. The price He paid was His own life! Jesus bled, suffered and died so you could live.

My Friend, open your heart and let Jesus fill it. Reach out and take hold of God's wonderful gift. This gift will change your life forever!

May God bless and keep
you in His loving arms.

Chapter 1

Why Am I Here?

By James Franklin Barber

Has this question, "Why Am I Here" ever crossed your mind? People have asked themselves this question countless times. We usually ask this, when something disastrous happens and shakes our world. Does God have a plan for our lives? Yes, God does, although we may not understand at the time what His plan is. One important thing for us to remember is that we must continually seek God in order for His plan to be fulfilled in our lives. God has given us all a special gift and He will make sure we use it for His glory.

Everyone needs to have a sense of why he or she is here on this earth. We need to know, we were created for a purpose. We will never find fulfillment and true happiness, until we are doing the things we were called to do for God. He won't move us into the big things, until we have been proven faithful in the small things. His lord said unto him, Well, done one good and faithful servant; thy has been faithful over a few things, I will make thee ruler over many things; enter thou into the joy of thy lord (Matthew 25:23). If now you are doing what you consider to be small things REJOICE because God is getting you ready for bigger things ahead.

One night, Carolyn and I were discussing God's Plan for our lives. I believe that God, even from the very beginning, had a special plan for my life. I was born on October 19, 1954 in Savanna, TN. I never knew anything about my natural parents. I was in foster care for about 2 years. One of my earliest memories was when I was a little boy living in a small house, which was surrounded by cotton. Late each afternoon, a man riding on a freight train, would wave and blow the whistle at me.

Frank and Ruby Barber from South Fulton, TN, adopted me at the age of 4. I know that God especially handpicked my parents for me. I could not have asked for a better mom and dad to share my life with. They needed a little boy and I needed a godly mom and dad. The memory of the man, on the train, had stayed with me for many years. My dad and I were talking one day about things, which had happened in the past. He said he remembered riding the freight train and seeing a little skinny, blond-haired boy, standing on his front porch. He remembered how happy it made the little boy, when he waved and blew the train whistle at him. I told my dad I believed with my whole heart, he was the man on the train and I was the little boy. It was all part of God's Plan for my life.

I never thought being adopted would be an issue with my family, until I experienced the events of the past 6 years. After my dad died in March

2007, my so-called family drastically changed their attitude toward me. All of my cousins, except one, treated me like an outsider instead of part of the family. They did everything possible, under the sun, to keep me from inheriting my parent's money. They knew my mom had Alzheimer disease and they saw their chance to take advantage of it. One day when she wasn't thinking clearly, they took her to their lawyer's office and got her to sign papers, taking my power of attorney away from me. Later she realized what she had done but it was too late to do anything about it. Shortly after this they came over to the trailer, where we were living and offered me $5,000.00 to have nothing else to do with my mom. It made me very furious for them to think I would do this to my mom. I couldn't believe that they would sink that low, but when you are dealing with money there is no limit to what they will do. They even had the nerve to accuse me of stealing a lot of money from my mom and dad. I have always heard it told, that the guilty dog barks the loudest. This is evidently true because while they were accusing me of stealing my dad's money, his gun and coin collection, all the tools in his workshop and his van mysteriously disappeared. I have no proof they took it all, but the circumstantial evidence is overwhelming. They were successful in what they had first planned to do six years ago. The house, a few acres of land and a small amount of money were the only things that were left for me after the death of my parents. There is a deep hurt still lingering inside of me because of the way my family, to whom I once was very close, treated me. After the death of my parents, I haven't had any contact with my cousins in over a year.

The strange thing is Carolyn's family has accepted me as a member of the family. Carolyn has one daughter named Stacy and two grandsons named Cody and Cameron. I have a son named Jordan. When Carolyn and I got married, we joined forces with Stacy and Jordan and became one family. We do not believe in the word "Step". I am a dad figure to Carolyn's daughter and I am better known as Paw Paw by her two sons.

Now that I'm an adult, I would like to know at least the medical history of my biological family but despite all my efforts to find my real mother or dad, I have not been able to get any information regarding her. After a lot of praying, I have decided not to go any farther with it. I have also decided, instead of worrying about my blood family, to focus on my ready-made family with Carolyn.

My friend, I agree that it would be beneficial to know your family's medical history, but keep in mind, not knowing your birth parents might not be a bad thing. If you were adopted at a young age by godly parents, please count your blessings. I am not saying, that you might not be curious, about whom your birth parents were, but do not end up concentrating so much on them, that you end up pushing your adopted parents away. Being adopted does not make you any less of a person; in fact it makes you a specially chosen individual.

God Bless You,
James Franklin Barber

Chapter 2

God's Plan For Our Lives

After the death of my late husband, I promised myself I would never get married again. I never thought I could love anyone else, but when I meet Jim in 2005, things changed for me. Brian and Tina Nichols, two of our closest friends, arranged a blind date for us to go to church with them. Jim and I meet on a Saturday and four days later we were married. We knew in our hearts that it was God that brought us together. We shared two main interests, which were our love for God and our desire to sing for Him. Our heart's desire was to serve God, but we had not fully surrendered our lives to Him to be used, as He wanted. We were holding on to this thing call "flesh." Jim and I wanted things to happen the way we wanted them to and on our time schedule. Self, instead of God, seemed to be first in our lives. We had a few rough edges God needed to work on, before He could use us in His ministry. One way or the other, God was going to get our attention!

The first time my mom met Jim, she fell in-love with him. She had Alzheimer disease and it was slowly pulling her down mentally and physically. Jim would stand by her bedside and sing Amazing Grace to her, which she loved dearly. Prior to meeting Jim, Stacy, my daughter was living with mom and me.

After we got married, Jim and I, with my mom's blessing, decided to move to South Fulton to live. Stacy told me she would stay there and take care of her granny. Jim and I would try to go back to Friendship every chance we could to help care for my mom. We also would attend church and practice our gospel singing.

Mom got to a point she had to have 24-hr medical attention and placing her in a nursing home was the only option we had. We sat down with the nurses and discussed what we were going to have to do concerning her. I never thought I would have to do this to my mom but I had no choice because I couldn't give her the medical care she needed. In February 2006, she had her first blood clot in the brain. She pulled through it but it damaged her brain and her heart. She was in a coma for two month. In addition to the Alzheimer disease, she had EDS (Ehlers Danlos Syndrome), which weakened the blood vessels in her heart. In June 2006, she had a second blood clot in the brain. This time there was no hope for her. I knew in my heart it was a matter of time death's door would open and she would enter in. I stayed by her side, holding her hand until she took her last breath. I hated to let my mom go but she was finally at peace. All of her suffering was over and she was with Jesus and my dad. I lost my best friend that day.

After the death of my mom, we moved Stacy, along with Cody and Cameron, our grandsons, to our home in South Fulton, TN. We were all living in Jim's doublewide trailer. It seemed that everything was working out for us, until Jim lost his job and couldn't find another one in the area. Our bills started piling up and with no money coming in, we had no way to pay them.

Sooner or later we were going to have to make some decisions as to what to do. I had inherited my late mother's home in Friendship, TN. so Jim and I had thought about moving there, because the living expenses would be less. Stacy, my daughter, who was living with us at the time, said if we decided to move to Friendship, that she would assume the responsibility for the bills at our home in South Fulton. The thought of moving seventy-five miles away from her and my two grandsons was breaking my heart. Reluctantly, we left South Fulton, headed to our home in Friendship, TN, with our clothes, a few pieces of furniture and an uncertain future.

We moved to Friendship, in the fall of 2008. Even though Jim had no job and we had been forced to leave our home in South Fulton, we still had church and the singing group, so we thought! The singing group that we were trying to establish didn't work out and it seemed to us that God had put our singing on the back burner. We got it in our heads that it was God's will for us to leave the church, which we were attending. Thinking back, I really don't know the reason why we left the church but I know it was a mistake on our part. Sometimes as Christians, we misinterpret our own will as being what God's will is. What we think might be the leading of the Holy Spirit may not be from Him at all but just our own thinking. When this happens, from time to time, we will make mistakes, but God loves us enough to forgive us. 1 John 1:9 tells us if we confess our sins, He is faithful and just to forgive us *our* sins, and to cleanse us from all unrighteousness.

The temperature during the Autumn season was pleasant for us, but it wasn't long, until we started feeling the chilling cold of winter. Sometimes it would get so cold in our home, that you could actually see your breath. We only had a couple of wall heaters to keep us warm, but despite that, we made it through the long winter with a lot of prayer and God's help. Thank God it wasn't long until old-man winter started fading away and spring was in the air. The spring season was comfortable for us, but we were soon to experience the sweltering heat of summer. We had no air-conditioning to keep us cool and only two fans to keep the hot air stirring. There were times, when the temperature in our home would get so high that it melted all of candles. I do admit there were times we had to ask God for strength to carry on. I'm sorry to say, from time to time, our old flesh gave down, which caused a hopeless feeling to come over the two of us. Our spirits were strong but our flesh was very weak. I can truthfully say we went through some very hot and miserable days and nights, but thank God, we made it through that long summer of 2009.

Later on that year, after working on the book one Thursday night, I woke up the next morning feeling good. Jim needed to go to Alamo, TN, so I decided to ride with him. It was a good time for me to go to the doctor and get refills on my medicine. As I walked into the doctor's office, I could see sick people all around me, but I didn't think much about it. My plan was to walk in, see the doctor and leave. My plan got changed big time! My short visit turned into over three hours.

After leaving the doctor's office, we went to the drug store and got my medicine and headed home. We wanted to do a few things before night set in. By 5 o'clock that afternoon, I started feeling dizzy, sick at my stomach and running a high fever. I told Jim I didn't want anything for supper and I was just going to go to bed. The next morning I was so sick I couldn't get out of bed. I called for Jim, but couldn't find him. Little did I know he was in the other bedroom, as sick as I was. He was only a door away, yet he couldn't come to me and I couldn't go to him. We didn't have a house phone at the time and the cell phone wouldn't pick up inside the house. We had no way to contact anyone to come and see about us. We went for three and a half days without food and very little to drink. Jim managed to get up long enough to get him some Mountain Dew and some tea for me.

As I lay there, I realized I had no one but God to help me. On the 4th day, I started feeling a little better but was still too sick to sit up. The only thing I could do was to lie in the bed and think. I was experiencing some emotions and thoughts that I had never felt before. I even thought of taking a handful of pain pills and ending it all. I had gone until I couldn't go any longer. All at once I cried out, "God, what is going on? I don't understand what is happening to us." At that moment of time, I lay there and cried, because I felt so powerless, helpless and so alone. It took me a few minutes to get my thoughts together and then I realized that I couldn't go any farther on my own. My strength was gone! I asked God to forgive me and help me go on in His strength. It was at that moment I surrendered everything to God.

Psalm 46:1 . . . God is our refuge and strength, a very present help in trouble. We all have or will have times when we feel completely powerless and helpless in the face of our circumstances. It's during these times God will be the only source of strength to get you through. Without God, we can't stand strong in the face of all that opposes us. We want to be an over comer not just a survivor! With

God beside us, we can overcome anything. We want a sense of purpose in our lives and we want to abound in God's love and blessings. We can never achieve that quality of life outside of the power of God. The only way to release that power is to totally surrender to God.

Some things are beyond us, bigger than us, greater than us, higher than our faith and deeper than our believing. God is going to say, in those instances, I am going to go beyond human ability and faith and display to everyone that I am God. God can do greater things than our minds eye can conceive or our hearts can believe, because,

God Is Still God.

God still speaks. God still heals. God still fills. God still answers prayer. God still sets free. God still saves. Be encouraged friend, God is still in the business of working miracles today!

Chapter 3

My Second Chance At Life

I had been diagnosed with EDS (Ehlers Danlos Syndrome), which is an inherited disorder that affects your connective tissues primarily your skin, muscles, joints and the blood vessel walls. I have had twelve surgeries, including two total knee replacements, due to EDS. Everyone has dreams they want to see fulfilled. I am holding onto all my dreams. My health problems are not going to keep me down or out. I am more determined to see my dreams fulfilled.

I hadn't had any problems with my heart, until the summer of 2010. I started feeling run down and began having problems with my legs swelling. I decided, that I needed to go to the doctor and see what was wrong. The nurse practitioner told me that my heart and blood pressure were normal and gave me a B12 shot. The two grandsons had been visiting that week, so we decided the next day we would take them home. I guess it was around 6:00 o'clock, when we arrived at my daughter's house in South Fulton. A couple of her friends came by, so Jim and I decided we would stay inside, while they were there. I was watching the T.V. while Jim was sitting at the computer checking his e-mail. All of a sudden the door flew open and in came my son-in-law. He told

Jim to get off the computer right then! Jim thought he was kidding, so he kept sitting there. The longer Jim sat at the computer, the madder my son-in-law got.

I couldn't believe the way we were being treated by him. There were some of the most ungodly words coming out of his mouth. This wasn't the first time he had done this to us. The first time it happened I overlooked it and forgave him. This time the way he was acting toward us was upsetting me, so I told Jim to get all our things together and we were going home. It seemed every time we came to visit them, he would get angry with us, without any reason at all.

I thought it would be best, if I walked outside and cooled down. After thinking about what had happened, I turned around and started walking back up the stairs when an excruciating pain hit me in my chest. By the time I got to the living room, the pain was so great, I couldn't get my breath.

My daughter saw what was happening and called 911. They arrived and took my blood pressure, which was very high. They said they needed to take me, as quickly as possible to the nearest hospital, which was located in Fulton, KY. The doctor, who was on call, said I needed to stay in the hospital to make sure I was ok. The next day the doctor came into my room and told me my heart rate had dropped to forty beats per minute, when I was awake and thirty beats while sleeping. He said they were immediately transporting me, by ambulance, to the Cardiac Unit at Western Baptist Hospital in Paducah, KY, a town about fifty miles from my daughter's home.

The next two days, the nurses monitored my heart rate and blood pressure. The doctor came in on Monday, July 1st, 2010 and told me, that I needed a pacemaker implanted to regulate my heart rate. I know, that God was with me all the way. He worked through the doctors to make my surgery a success. The day after my surgery, I was able to leave the hospital and go home. Later during one of my return doctor's visits, I was told, that if I had left my daughter's and gone home, I would have died. It put a scare in me, when I was told how close to death I had been. I realized, that material things weren't that important to me anymore. You can always replace those things, but if you loose your life, you have lost it all.

God can take the bad and make something good come from it. I became aware of my heart problem, because of my son-in-laws mistakes. God's ways are not our ways and His thoughts are not our thoughts. For my thoughts are not your thoughts, neither are your ways my ways, says the Lord. (Isaiah 55:8). I knew, in my heart, that I had to forgive my son-in-law for his actions, but forgiveness is never easy. When we forgive someone, it doesn't make him or her right, nor does it justify what he or she has done, but it simply releases him or her into God's hands, so He can deal with them. Forgiveness is actually the best revenge, because it not only sets us free, from the person we forgive, but it frees us to move into all God has for us. God says, Be kind to one another, tenderhearted, forgiving one another, just as God in Christ forgave you (Ephesians 4:31). Often we don't recognize the unforgiveness that we are harboring in us. We think we are forgiving someone, but we really aren't. If we don't ask God to reveal our unforgiveness to us, we may never get free of the paralyzing grip it has on our lives. A big part, of making sure our lives are clean and right before God, has to do with forgiving other people. We can never move into all God has for us, unless we do. When we choose to forgive, not only do we benefit, but also do the people around us.

No sin, action or choice on your part is too big for God to handle, or too big to be worked for the good of those who love Him and are the called according to his purpose. (Romans 8:29) You can embrace the present, because the past is gone, and no energy you expend will ever change it. The future is in God's hands, so you're free to focus on the present. Your desire should be to love God with all your heart, soul and mind, trusting Him to forgive the past and transform your future.

Martyred missionary Jim Eliot once wrote, "Wherever you are, be all there—not living in the past and not fantasizing about the future." God wants you in the present, because that's where his Grace will flow. You can look toward the future, because even if you make mistakes today, God still controls the future. Walking in the Spirit, you can live life to its fullest, unafraid of making mistakes and unconcerned that you may stumble into some terrible circumstance, of which God has no control.

Even when things appear to be going the wrong way in your life, you can trust, that God is busy working out His divine plan through you. Look for God's hand in every situation in your life. Walk by faith and know, that God's hand is stretched out to you, even in your most difficult times. You can trust His ability and His willingness to change the bad things into the good. God is not limited by people's motives. In other words, it doesn't matter why someone hurts you, God still can transform a mean-spirited situation into something for his or her good. So whatever trial, situation, problem or struggle comes your way, intentionally or unintentionally, remember they will serve an amazing purpose, whether we are aware of it at the time or not. Trials will allow us to grow and truly experience the magnificence of the human being that we are. You only have to rise to the occasion that is presented before you and release the power and the ability that is within you, to turn something bad into something good.

Chapter 4

Calm Before The Storm

Jim and I had been through many trials and struggles over the last five years. Little did we know this had been the calm before the storm! We decided to go to South Fulton for the Mothers Day weekend in 2011. I thought Stacy and I could enjoy the weekend together. We arrived at her house around 9 o'clock Saturday morning. She had very little to say to us the whole day. On Mother's Day, she got up mad about something. I don't know what it was! I didn't want to cause any problem so I stayed out of her way and left her alone. She called two of her friends to come over for hamburgers and hot dogs. Everything was peaches and cream between her and her friends, but she completely ignored Jim and me. Not once did she tell me "Happy Mother's Day" and this hurt me very deeply!

All at once she jumped up and started swearing and calling me names. She told me she wished I would get my things and go home, so that's what we did. We gathered up our things and told the boys we loved them and left. My heart felt like it broke into pieces, because of how I had been treated on this very special day. It had been the worst Mothers Day I had ever experienced. I felt in my spirit, that something wasn't right, because of the way she acted, especially in front of her friends. I cried so much on the way home I fell asleep. The next evening, when Jim came home from work, he asked me if I had heard from Stacy. He said he felt, in his spirit, that something bad was going to happen. He and I agreed that something wasn't right in South Fulton.

May 11, 2011, will remain in our memories for the rest of our lives. Six weeks prior to this I had fallen and broken my hand. I had gone for a check-up that day to see how my hand was doing. Jim and I decided to stop on the way home and to get a bite to eat for supper. We were sitting there talking when all at once Jim said he felt we needed to get home as soon as possible. When we arrived home. I heard the phone ringing as I started up the steps, Jim unlocked the door for me and I hurried in to answer it. Neither of us realized how much this phone call would dramatically changed our lives over the next 2 years. The voice on the other end was Cody, our oldest grandson, crying, "Nana, please come as soon as you can, cause they have arrested mama and Peanut." I took a few minutes to collect my thoughts because I couldn't believe what I had just heard! I hollered at Jim to come as quickly as he could because we had to go to South Fulton immediately. We grabbed a few things and started on our 75 mile—trip. There was silence between us all the way because neither of us could believe what we had just heard from Cody. I told Jim to pinch me to see if I was asleep or awake because it felt like a bad dream to me.

As we drove up the long driveway to the trailer, all we could see were flashing blue lights and drug enforcement officers all over the place. We looked at each other and asked the question, "What's going on." One cop pulled us to the side and told us, that my daughter and her husband had been arrested for manufacturing and the intent to sell Methamphetamines. He said he was glad we came, because he didn't want to call Children Services to pick up the boys.

They finally left around 10:30 that night, leaving the trailer turned upside down. They pulled everything out of the closets and dresser drawers, especially in Stacy and Peanut's room. They broke a door, turned over chairs, pulled pictures off the walls and did other damage to the trailer. The next day we had to go to Juvenile Court to petition for temporary custody of our two grandsons, Cody and Cameron. We were still in shock because of all the things that had taken place over the last 24 hours.

We had to come up with over $600.00 to cover Stacy's bills for the month. It took all the money we had saved up to pay them. Jim had a good job working at AKC Janitorial Services, but unfortunately he had to give it up because it was too far away. The only money coming in was my disability check of $685.00 a month and it wasn't enough to take care of the four people living in the home. Yes, I admit I started worrying about things. What were we doing to do? We couldn't get any kind of government assistance, because I owned the house in Friendship. It seemed no one wanted to help us. Our bad dream had just become a terrible nightmare.

While my daughter was in jail, I could see a small change in her. She had started going to church, reading her bible and was even baptized. Every time we would go to visit her, she was so nice to me. She would tell me that she loved me. "I LOVE YOU" are precious words to any mother.

There were several times Stacy had to appear before the judge. Each time I saw her wearing chains and handcuffs, my heart would break into. I couldn't believe how much weight she had lost. As we sat in the courtroom, we listened to the judge call each case before him. Over 85% of the cases were drug related and many of them were dealing with the manufacturing and sale of Meth. The ages of the defendants ranged from 16 to 50. One case in particular, which stood out to us was dealing with seven members of the same family. They were all being charged with the same offense as our daughter, Stacy.

JIM AND CAROLYN BARBER

This is something I don't want any family to go through. I thought I knew my child, but I was so blinded to the fact of what she was doing. This could happen to your child, brother, sister even mom or dad. If you love them, please take the blinders off and see the warning signs.

She was released from jail on August 8, 2011 and placed in drug court under supervision based on frequent drug testing and classroom appearances. The first week everything seemed to be going all right with her. I knew she was going through some off times, trying to adjust to a life, without drugs. Her behavior seemed to change overnight, back into the Stacy I didn't like. She started getting mad over every little thing. She started having resentment toward Jim. Why, I don't know! I didn't understand why she was treating him this way, after all the things he had done for her. It didn't matter what it was, she would fly off the handle and start cursing and calling him names. I know she was dealing with things, but she needed to understand that we were dealing with things too. I admit we had a few problems with her, but there was nothing we could do but give it to God.

Jim finally found a job working at Pizza Hut. The pay wasn't great but it was a little money coming in. We had gotten behind on our van payments. Late one night, they came and repossessed it, leaving us with no transportation. Jim had to quit his job because he had no way to get to it. This meant no job-no transportation—no transportation-no job. Stacy wouldn't let us borrow her car to go anywhere not even the doctor. If Jim needed to go anywhere, he would have to walk a mile to catch the city transit van or ask someone else to take him. We both felt like we were prisoners behind imaginary bars.

Before the repossession of our van, we had started attending a church in South Fulton, TN. The people seemed friendly but with our Pentecostal background, the services were so much different, from what we were use to. Shortly after we started attending the church we had to ask them for help with our light bill and some food. Jim filled out an application hoping to get approved. Two men from the Benevolence Committee came to our home to see if we qualified to get our light bill paid. One of the men started asking personal questions and making cruel statements to us. I couldn't believe what I was hearing! The first thing he said to us was that we made a mistake moving to South Fulton to take care of our grandsons. He said he wouldn't do it for anybody! His cruel words made me start crying. He said, "I know I have upset you, but I thought you needed to know."

My daughter came into the room to talk to the men. Our grandsons were in another part of the house, listening to what was being said. He started talking about the houses that he rented out and he looked at us and said, "You know I wouldn't rent my houses to people like you." I thought to myself "people like you!" The man's words kept ringing in my ears until I got really upset. What made me so mad was the fact that these so-called Christians were treating us this way. There was no compassion from either of the two men. I asked myself, "WHERE WAS THE LOVE OF GOD?"

For days the words of this man kept reverberating deep down in my inner being and the ill feelings continued toward him. I didn't like the feelings I was experiencing at the time, so I started talking to God. I asked God to forgive me and to take those feelings out of my heart. I told God I never wanted to treat anyone, like these men had treated us. We reached out for help to people, who called themselves "Christians," but received none. I asked God, "Where was the love of God in these people?" God spoke to me and said, "They know of Me but they don't know Me." A feeling of sadness came over me and I started praying for God to help these men to realize where they had been wrong, so they could get things right with Him.

If you haven't experience being hurt by someone at church, it's likely one of the worst pains you will ever feel. To think, the one you thought could help you or offer encouragement is the one who ends up kicking you, when you are down. The church is supposed to be the one place, where you are safe, people are accepting, forgiving and free from conflict and pain. There are some churches however, where some elements of strife, conflict, jealousy and hatred, have crept into the congregation and caused them to forget what their real purpose is. They live with blinders on, not seeing the needs and hurts of people. Jim and I have been guilty of the same thing in the past, but the experience of what we have gone through changed our views, concerning the needs of others. I pray, that it never happens to you but if it does, please don't write God off, because of the way His children act. God loves us and would never do that to us. Don't blame God! There are still good people out there, who are dedicated, spirit-filled, loving and forgiving.

We knew in our hearts, coming to South Fulton to take care of our grandsons was right thing to do. I couldn't understand why all this was happening to us. Jim left his job that he loved so much and we had to leave our home, our church and our friends in Friendship. It seemed because of our doing what was right, that bad things were happening to us. We couldn't get any help, our van was repossessed, and we were cussed out and called ungodly names, like "White Trash and moochers." I admit that my faith got weak and I asked many times "WHY?' What had we done to deserve all of this? There was an anger and resentment building up in me. I know that Jim and I caused the trials in the past, but this time we didn't deserved what was happening to us.

God showed me that when we give place to anger, bitterness and resentment it shuts off all He has for us in our lives. Just when God is moving in our lives in a powerful way, we give in to anger and completely shut Him off. I knew I was guilty of this and I asked God to keep me from having all these negative feelings so Jim and I could remain in the flow of what He had in store for us.

UPDATE: Thank You, Jesus!! Stacy and Seburn, her husband, are out of jail now. Stacy has graduated from drug court at the top of her class. While she was in drug court, all of her drug tests came back negative. They both have good jobs and have remained clean and sober for twenty-four months now. Stacy and I are closer than we have been in a long time. Jim and I decided to stay in South Fulton so we could be with our family. We all live in the same yard so I get to see her and the boys almost everyday. Jordan lives a mile away so we get to see him too.

Chapter 5

Who Are You?

(Coping With Alzheimer Disease)

This chapter is dedicated to our moms:

Wilsie Lee Jackson

Born: Jan. 15, 1923

Died: June 6, 2006

Ruby Lee Barber

Born: April 27, 1918

Died: Dec.20, 2011

"For Everything There Is A Season . . .
A Time To Be Born, and A Time To Die."
—Ecclesiastes 3:1-2

Jim and I felt it was time for Stacy to assume her responsibilities caring for the boys and her home. We had prayed that God would lead us to make the right decision, concerning where to move. We wanted to move back to Friendship, TN. but our hearts were telling us to stay here in South Fulton.

Jim's mom had been dealing with Alzheimer for some time now and it had gotten to the point, that the sitters who were staying with her couldn't handle her anymore. We prayed and made the decision to move in and take care of her. My mom had Alzheimer disease and died with it in 2006. Having already been through this with my mom, we knew what road we were about to travel with Jim's mom. He had been there for me and now I could be there for him.

I am not saying dealing with Jim's mother's illness had been easy because it had not. At times, the stress and fatigue got to me and I had to step back, shed a few tears and go on. Jim and I felt this was another chapter in our lives. There are so many families that are dealing with this dreaded disease called Alzheimer.

Alzheimer disease is a process, in which brain tissue steadily degenerates, decreasing the brain's function over time, which causes memory loss and some mental disabilities. Alzheimer disease is physically and mentally draining for both an Alzheimer's patient as well as her family. It is also very hard to take on the role as the caregiver; because of the way Alzheimer's affects the patient's memory.

It can be very frustrating when caring for somebody who has this disease, because it causes temperament issues with the patient. In addition, sometimes sufferers possess memory loss so severe, that they forget whom you are and become very frightened. It would greatly benefit you as a family member or caregiver, to research this disease and try to understand the effects that come from it. By doing this, you'll have an easier time realizing, why the patient does certain things or acts certain ways. In turn, you will have a much easier time deciding the appropriate actions to improve the situation.

People with Alzheimer's are people first. They need to be encouraged, have a sense of value and most of all need to be treated with dignity and sincere love. Many feelings come up when dealing with someone, who has this awful disease. Sometimes caring for your stricken loved one forces you to examine yourself and your life. It invites you to revisit this particular relationship with your loved one mindfully, openly and respectfully as you become aware that the past cannot be changed.

Be open and be prepared for anything to happen. Try to stay calm and relaxed. When your loved one sees you are calm and comfortable, they pick up on that mood as well. Smile and let them know you are happy to be with them.

On December 20, 2011, Ms. Ruby went to be with JESUS. A couple of months before her death

Jim and I moved in to take care of her. She was sitting in a chair, eating three small meals a day and loved talking about her childhood. She couldn't remember the present, but she would talk about her twin brother, Rufee, who had passed on and frequently talked on the phone to Mildred, her only living sister. As each day passed, she ate less and less, her talking was more confused and little by little she became weaker. She soon got to a point she couldn't sit up anymore by herself. The only way to give her water or Ensure was through a syringe. There were times she couldn't swallow anything. Truthfully, she had lost so much weight she looked like a skeleton. As I sit by her bed I often wondered what Jim and I had done wrong. Could we have done anything to keep her from getting to this point? One day a nurse, from Hospice, sat me down and talked to me. She told me that we were doing all we could do for Miss Ruby. She went on to say she was in her final stage of Alzheimer's and there was nothing anyone could do for her, except to keep her comfortable.

Two days before she died, I came in to check on her and she started talking coherently, just like she had, before contracting the disease. I called for Jim to come into the living room and told him there was someone I wanted him to meet. I told him THIS IS YOUR MAMA! She knew who he was, who I was and talked about things surrounding her. Jim was sitting on one side and I was sitting on the other talking and enjoying that time together. This precious time lasted about ten minutes and then she slipped off into a deep sleep. All at once she opened her eyes pointed to the ceiling and said "IT'S SO BEAUTIFUL" then paused for a second and said "JESUS." Suddenly, she was surrounded by a bright glow and had the biggest smile on her face. We knew she had seen JESUS. It wasn't long until she drifted into a deep sleep. Each breath she took seemed like the last one she would take. I decided that I would sit beside her bed so she wouldn't be alone when she died. I knew in my heart, that we would soon be saying goodbye to her. We were watching her walk toward death's door. There is no easy way to say a last goodbye to your love one.

If someone you love is dying, the weeks or months ahead hold much pain, but they can also hold the makings of warm memories. Good byes are tough, no question. Remembering the good times and the love we shared helped us through our good byes to our moms. A dying person will slip from your grip no matter how tightly you cling to them, but some things can be held tightly only with open hands—and a loving heart. Hold your hands wide open to receive a treasury of stored memories, which includes the love you and your loved one shared together. My friend, there is someone who never grips too tightly and yet will never let go. God is that someone. God will never leave you nor forsake you. Hebrews 13:5-6 for He has said, 'I will never leave you, nor forsake you,' so that we may boldly say, 'The Lord is my helper, and I will not fear what man shall do to me."

Many, if not most, of us have probably been in physical need at some time. All of us are in spiritual need, and will remain that way as long as we live in this body of flesh with its carnal nature. But God does not abandon us. NEVER!! We can always trust in Him to be there for us, no matter how hard and how far we fall. The word "never" in this passage is from "ou we," in Greek what is known as an empathetic negative. In other words, "never" means just that. NEVER!!!!!

Miss Me, But Let Me Go

When I come to the end of the road,

The sun has set for me.

I want no rites and a gloomy filled room,

Why cry for a soul set free.

Miss me a little . . .

But not too long

And not with you head bowed low.

Remember the love that once was shared.

Miss me . . . But let me go.

For this is a journey we all must take

And each must go alone.

It's all a part of the Masters Plan,

A step on the road to home.

When you are lonely and sick in heart,

Go to God we know

And bury your sorrows in doing good deeds

Miss me . . . But let me go.

-Author Unknown-

Chapter 6

Surrendering It All To God

When I was young I asked Jesus to come into my heart to live. I always went to church with my mom and dad every Sunday. I grew up knowing Jesus, learning all of the Bible stories and memorizing them. I was known as a good girl, who told others about Jesus, followed all of the rules, to the best of my ability and tried to do all that was expected of me. As I matured into adulthood, there was something missing in my heart. The peace I thought was supposed to be there wasn't. I tried to fill that void with drugs and alcohol. It had gotten to a point, where I was emotionally out of control and felt I had nothing left inside. I had no clue, who Carolyn was or where to turn. In the process, I was hurting everyone around me.

One night, after the death of my 2nd husband in 1997, I realized how empty and out of control I was. I poured my heart out and surrender to God. I told Him how I felt, and how I had messed things up, trying to do it my own way. I asked for forgiveness and promised Him, that if I lived another day, every breath I took and every day I lived would belong to Him. I couldn't do it my way anymore, so I had to let go and give God charge of my life.

When I think back to that night in 1997, I realize now I hadn't given God full control of my life. For sixteen years, I thought I was right with God and that I had surrendered everything to Him. God chose those three and half days, that Jim and I were so sick to show me how powerless, helpless and alone I was. I didn't realize that God was speaking to both, Jim and me at the same time. On the 4th day of our sickness, we both totally surrendered our hearts, bodies and souls to God. It was the first day of the rest of our lives with Him.

Since then, our lives have been a continuous state of change and growth. We are learning step-by-step to truly trust God and allow Him to have full control of our lives, home, family and finances. We are learning what love, joy and peace truly mean.

The word "surrender" is defined as: to yield, give up or over, submit, abandon, relinquish, cede, waive, or capitulate. In some translations, the word "surrender" is not found, but the concepts of "yielding"(Romans 6:16-19) or submitting (James 4:7) is used instead.

Surrendering to God involves a relationship, and this relationship involves trust and faith for our lives. By surrendering to God, we let go of whatever has kept us from wanting God's ways first. Surrendering everything means being willing to say,

"God, whatever You want me to do, I'll do it." Yes, to anything, You ask of me, even if it means dying to my desires and myself. I will give up the things I want to do in order to have more of You in my life. God, I will put You first and give total submission to You."

What is submission? Submission is something you decide to do, not something someone forces you to do. The meaning of the word "submit" is to submit yourself. It's a condition of the heart. Having a submitted heart means you are willing to give all of yourself and come into proper alignment with God's will.

A thought comes to my mind about an old western movie, where the good guy points his gun at the bad guy and says, "Stick um up." The bad guy drops his gun, raises his hands and says, "I give up." This is the kind of surrender God wants. Truthfully, we aren't the bad guys and God isn't pointing a gun at us, but rather He is pointing His finger at us in a loving way and saying, "My child, I want you to give me all and give me everything. I have so much that I want to give back to you." We need to drop everything and say, "God, I give up! I totally surrender to You my all. Please take my life and use it as You want and I will do whatever You say."

If we would do this, our lives would be so much better. Believe me, I know! Why is it so hard for us to do this Is because we want, what we want and were afraid of what, God might ask us to do, if we surrender. We doubt, that God only asked us to do things for Him, because He wants us to be on His winning team.

A person has to surrender their mind, body and soul to God. This is often the toughest part of surrendering. Romans 6:13 says, "Do not offer the parts of your body to sin, as instruments of wickedness, but rather offer yourselves to God, as those who have been brought from death to life; and offer the parts of your body to Him as instruments of righteousness."

To surrender heart, body, and soul to God, one must understand that as humans we are triune (three part) beings. We are made up of our mind, body, and soul. Yielding one part of ourselves, without yielding the other is impossible. When we try to separate these three parts of our being, we become "double minded" and therefore unstable (James 1:8). However, the initial surrender is only the beginning. The surrender of your mind, body, and soul to God is an ongoing process, that begins the moment one is born again as a child of God and it continues, until He calls the believer home or Jesus comes again. The process is one of growing in grace and knowledge of God and that comes from studying the Word of God and choosing to apply divine viewpoints to your life on a daily, sometimes moment-by-moment basis.

The eternal destination, of a man's soul is determined by, which of the two following choices he makes. The first is to reject God, which causes eternal separation from Him. If you don't accept Jesus, here on earth, as your personal Savior, (1 John 14: 6), your soul will be separated from God, in HELL for eternity. The second choice is to accept Jesus, live the abundant life and abide with Him forever in Heaven. You will have fellowship and communication with God, through Jesus Christ, during your life and will then enjoy His presence for eternity.

My friend, if you are struggling with total surrender to God, talk to Him about your thoughts, feelings, and resistance. Surrendering to God means that we yield our ownership to Him. We relinquish control of our time, property, career or anything that we consider as rights to God. We acknowledge, what we thought was ours, is actually God's. We are simply caretakers of what God has given us. We acknowledge that He knows best and we want His perfect plan in our lives!

It is wonderful what miracles God works in wills that are utterly surrendered to Him. He turns hard things into easy, and bitter things into sweet. It is not that He puts easy things in the place of the hard, but He actually changes the hard things into easy ones.

Chapter 7

Patience

One thing that we have had a problem with through our difficult times is patience. We are learning, that God's ways are not our ways and His thoughts are not our thoughts. "For my thoughts are not your thoughts, neither are your ways my ways, saith the Lord" (Isaiah 55:8). We are learning, that Gods timing is not our timing. God is always doing more, than we can see through our physical eyes, so we have to trust Him, regardless of how long He takes to bring it to pass. God perfects and refines us, before He brings us into all He has for us, and that takes time. "That ye be not slothful, but followers of them who through faith and patience inherit the promises." (Hebrews 6:12).

What is patience? Patience is being mild, gentle and constant in all circumstances. The real test of patience is not in waiting, but in how one acts, while he or she is waiting. A person, who has developed patience, will be able to put up with things, without losing his or her temper. Scripture tells us in (James 1:4), But let patience have her perfect work, that ye may be perfect and entire, wanting (lacking) nothing. Reaching this point is definitely a process, which takes a lot of faith and trust in God. However, we can learn to enjoy life where we are, while we are waiting, for what we desire.

Another word for patience is long-suffering. Long-suffering bears something, yea, many things, without seeking to be avenged by word or act. Long-suffering is patience with offense, coupled together with long endurance. If you are long-suffering, you will not impart to others your supposed knowledge of your brother's mistakes and errors. You will seek to help and save him, because the blood of Jesus has purchased him. Long-suffering is not to be gloomy and sad, sour and hard hearted; it's to be exactly the opposite.—Ellen G. White, My Life Today.

Our patience and long-suffering with others should stem, at least partly, from our realization of Gods patience and long-suffering with us. Imagine if God treated each of us as we often treat another! Fortunately, He doesn't, and the fact, that He is exceedingly patient with our faults, and us means we should be patient with others and their faults. As we look in the mirror and see ourselves, for what we are and know that God loves and endures with us despite what we see in the mirror, we will be better able to truly manifest this fruit of long-suffering. In and of ourselves, we can't do it; but only through surrendering our will to His will, can we truly bear the fruits of patience and long-suffering in our own lives.

Five I Wills of Patience:

1. I will change the things I can change and accept the things I can't.

2. I will keep trying until I succeed.

3. I will make the most of my spare time.

4. I will not interrupt God's Plan for my life.

5. I will not complain if I don't get my own way.

How we demonstrate patience to God.

1. Thanking God during the trial, knowing that He is working through it, to build in me the character of Jesus Christ.

2. Serving others as unto the Lord even though there is no apparent gratitude or recognition for my service.

3. Obeying God by faith even though my natural inclinations tell me otherwise.

4. Allowing God the freedom to work rather than attempting to change people and situations in my own strength.

What new behavioral traits are needed for patience to develop in your life?

To increase your level of patience you need to:

1. Develop a consistent philosophy of life. Take life one day at a time. Consider each day as a gift of life, which will allow you to get one step closer to your goal of growth and change.

2. Accept the reality of your humanity in that you are going to need time, effort and energy to change and grow. You will experience some resistance to altering long-standing, habitual ways of acting, reacting and believing.

3. Reframe your perspective on the past, present, and future. Don't dwell on your past mistakes and failings. Don't worry about what you will become or how you will act in the future. Begin to live each new day as a fresh start.

4. Break larger goals down into components that are short-term goals and objectives, more realistically attainable in the immediate future.

5. Be systematic in planning your path to recovery and growth.

6. Accept, understand and forgive yourself for being fragile, imperfect and weak.

You need to become your own best friend and cheerleader. Love yourself! Wake up to the realities of life around you. Everyone, with whom you come in contact, is busy working through their own struggles, weaknesses, setbacks, relapses, crises and obstacles to their personal growth and recovery. All of us are on the path to personal growth. There is no one exempt from this journey. It takes a lifetime to complete.

It gets hard and very frustrating at times to find patience in all these trials and struggles of life. I am so thankful for Jim, my partner not only as a mate, but also as a brother in Jesus. Having a Christian mate makes all the difference in the world. I know we have a greater purpose in life, which is to serve God and do His perfect will. I believe that all things are possible through Him. Prayer is our best weapon against the world's negativity and the devil's continuous taunting. I pray for God's peace to allow all of us to show patience through all situations and that God's grace will be sufficient to sustain us through all things.

Chapter 8

Trusting God

Proverbs 3:5-8 . . . Trust in the Lord with all your heart and lean not on your own understanding; in all your ways acknowledge him, and He will make your paths straight. Do not be wise in your own eyes; fear the Lord and shun evil. This will bring health to your body and nourishment to your bones.

Like many Christians today, you may struggle to believe, that God will provide for your daily needs. Perhaps you're facing an overwhelmingly difficult trial that exhausts your resources. Perhaps you're wondering if He will ever fulfill your heart's desire in a particular area. Trusting the Lord means looking beyond what we can see to what God sees (David won the victory against Goliath, an experienced, intimidating warrior, because the young shepherd saw the conflict from his God's perspective.

Have you ever wished you had a stronger faith in God? When the storms of life come, do they seem to wash you out to sea, before you can't get your bearings or perspective Well, if that's the case, you're in good company, because I don't think there's anyone on this earth who can say with 100% assurance that they trust God perfectly in every area of their life. But the fact remains, that as a follower of Jesus Christ, our faith should make a difference. It's designed to be much more, than just a belief system.

All of life is about learning to know and trust God. Trust doesn't come naturally to any of us; trust has to be learned. In the same way we learn to trust our parents or other people in our lives, we must also learn to trust God. Learning to trust God seems to require learning to stop relying on yourself so much. It means radical change at the very core of our being. Most of us don't like change of any kind, much less surgery on our core—SELF. Surgery hurts; it incapacitates and can even make us howl with pain.

God, the divine surgeon, is worth trusting. He loves us more, than we can know. His wounding seems grievous, but He restores us to wholeness. Be still and learn to trust God while He is working on you! You will laugh again!

I believe this year has taught us the most value lesson of them all >>>TRUST<<<. God is our only source of taking care of our needs, whether it is physical, mental or spiritual. He does supply our resources, but at times we try to do it ourselves. Without a doubt, there will come a point in every Christian's life, when all of his or her resources have run out, causing that person to place their full trust in God.

One of the things, that helped me is, that I chose not to blame God, for the things we went through. A lot of people get stuck asking, "Why." Personally I have asked God many times, "WHY GOD, WHY" We are now beginning to understand why we had to go through all the things we did. We may never know "Why" we went through some of the things we did, until we cross over to the other side of eternity. I found a quote that really sticks in my mind. "God has a reason for allowing things to happen. We may never understand His wisdom but we simply have to trust His will."

I read the end of the book of Job, which demonstrates that God "is who He is." He surely doesn't have to answer to us. So many people get hung up in No-man's Land—demanding an explanation, instead of choosing to trust a God, who loves us and has the bigger picture in mind, for our lives. We simply have to trust His will!! Every challenge presents an opportunity, for God to display His faithfulness and love. Instead of yielding to thoughts of fear and failure, make a commitment to trust Him, even when you don't know what tomorrow will bring. Yes, you may experience failure, and life may not always turn out as you planned, but ultimately, God will be glorified, and you will be blessed.

Philippians 4:6-7 says, "Be anxious for nothing, but in everything by prayer and supplication with thanksgiving let your requests be made known to God. And the peace of God, which surpasses all comprehension, will guard your hearts and your minds in Christ Jesus."

Take your burden to the Lord in prayer. Thank Him for working on your behalf, and rest in His supernatural peace. When you place your trust in God, you tap into an unstoppable force that nothing and no one can successfully oppose.

Trusting God won't make the mountain smaller, but it will make the climbing easier. Do not ask God for a lighter load, but instead ask Him for a stronger back.

Chapter 9

Our Faith Is Under Attack

Faith is the striking force, of the power of God, in our lives. Faith is what storms the forts of the devil and invades the world of demonic power, which causes sickness, disease and sin. Faith in God releases the lightning power of God to deliver us. The gift of faith is imparted from God, through the Word, but the Holy Spirit produces the fruit of faith. The gift of faith can move mountains, but the fruit of faith is what is required for daily living. The fruit of faith enables us to walk and love by faith (Romans 5:2). Without this kind of faith, it's impossible to please God (Hebrews 11:6).

Faith is not a tangible material, that can be seen, heard, smelled, tasted or touched, but is as real as anything that can be perceived with these five senses. Faith is as certain as is the existence of water.

Faith is as sure as the taste of an apple, the fragrance of a rose, the sound of thunder, the sight of the sun, the feel of a loving touch. Hope is a wish, a longing for something, not yet possessed, but with the expectation of getting it. Faith adds surely to the expectation of hope.

Our faith in God is under fierce satanic attack. All the demons of hell, along with the devils principalities and powers of darkness are waging an all-out war against the faith of Gods saints. We wrestle not against flesh and blood, but against the rulers of darkness of this world, against wickedness in high places (Ephesians 6:12).

I do believe, that the devil has brought intense attacks against God's people, causing awful suffering. It says in John 10:10, that the devil has come as a thief to steal, kill and destroy. In today's world there is such an unprecedented barrage of sicknesses, afflictions, troubles and unending problems, that it seems impossible, for the believer, to live an overcoming life. Be sober, be vigilant; because your adversary the devil as a roaring lion walketh about seeking whom he may devour (1 Peter 5:8).

Why is the devil so determined to shake our faith in God? He knows, when our faith grows cold, that we will lose hope in God. He puts thoughts in our mind, such as "Where is your God now? Look how things are going from bad to worse, and your pain, your suffering and your needs keep mounting with no relief in sight. Your God promised to make a way of escape for you so where is He now, when you need Him most?" If you listen to satan, you'll begin to feel your faith being shaken and if you listen to him long enough, feelings of defeat will take over your life.

Jesus said unto them, "Because of your unbelief: for verily I say unto you, if ye have faith as a grain of mustard seed, ye shall say unto the mountain, remove hence to yonder place; and it shall remove and nothing shall be impossible unto you." (Matthew 17:20). If you have great faith, it is faith; if you have little faith-it is faith. If you will just release what faith you have whether big, middle-size, even little faith, then God can release his miracle-working power in your life.

Our faith may waiver, but we can still keep our eyes on Jesus. He is patient and merciful. He hears all our complaints and questions and He sees so many doubtful thoughts in our minds, yet He looks upon us with forgiveness and love. He says if we keep our eyes continually on Him, we will make it through whatever we face in this lives.

Dear friend, we as Christians (yes, this includes Jim and me) need to get off our lazy do-nothings and start exercising our God-given faith and simply introduce our small problems to "OUR BIG GOD" instead of our big problems to our small God.

Matthew `9:26 . . . . But Jesus beheld them, and said unto them, With Men this is impossible: but "WITH GOD ALL THINGS ARE POSSIBLE."

Hope is nothing more than the expectation of those things which faith has believed to be truly promised by God.

Chapter 10

Showing Compassion
In An Evil World

"For I was an hungered, and ye gave me meat: I was thirsty, and ye gave me drink: I was a stranger, and ye took me in: Naked, and ye clothed me: I was sick, and ye visited me: I was in prison, and ye came unto me. Then shall the righteous answer him, saying, Lord, when saw we thee an hungered, and fed thee or thirsty, and gave thee drink When saw we thee a stranger, and took thee in or naked, and clothed thee Or when saw we thee sick, or in prison, and came unto thee And the King shall answer and say unto them, Verily I say unto you, Inasmuch as ye have done it unto one of the least of these my brethren, ye have done it unto me. Then shall he say also unto them on the left hand, Depart from me, ye cursed, into everlasting fire, prepared for the devil and his angels: For I was hungered, and ye gave me no meat: I was thirsty, and ye gave me no drink: I was a stranger, and ye took me not in: naked, and ye clothed me not: sick, and in prison, and ye visited me not. Then shall they also answer him, saying, Lord, when saw we thee a hungered, or a thirst, or a stranger, or naked, or sick, or in prison, and did not minister unto thee Then shall he answer them, saying, Verily I say unto you, Inasmuch as ye did it not to one of the least of these, ye did it not to me. And these shall go away into everlasting punishment: but the righteous into life eternal."~Matthew 25:35-46 ~

Compassion is the desire to ease other people's suffering. Compassion is a sympathetic awareness of another's distress, combined with a desire to alleviate it. Compassion is shown through kindness and caring and through our service and generosity toward others. Compassion is actually feeling what another person is feeling. It's like empathy with sharing. The word empathy literally means 'to suffer together'.

Sympathy is a feeling of 'togetherness'. Compassion can make you sympathize (because you are literally in the same emotional boat), but it's not necessary, that you have any awareness of someone else's feelings, but only, that you can identify with the person on their own emotional level. Compassion, in my view, is neither empathy nor sympathy, alone, but requires both.

There is also no right way and no one-way ticket to experiencing compassion. Some feel it for themselves first, then for others after, or the feeling for another opens the floodgates inward and then pours it back out. It honestly doesn't matter, so long as over the course of our lives, we learn to show compassion, and observe this sweet negotiation between its loving flow in and out.

Jim, over the last year, has experienced compassion on a level very few will. He has shared with me, how he really had never shown a lot of compassion, for those sitting on the side of the road, having car troubles or having to stand in food lines in order to feed their families, until he experienced it first hand.

After the death of Jim's mother, we took what little money that was left and bought an older model car. In a few months, we starting having problems with it not wanting to start and sometimes it wouldn't run at all. We had no extra money to get the car fixed. Every time he left the house, Jim would step out in faith and go ahead and drive it not knowing whether it would run or not. He always prayed before he left, that God would make a way to get there and back. We had no one, but God to depend on for help. One day, after picking up a few things at the grocery store, Jim pulled out of the parking lot onto the main street, where the car went dead. He tried over and over to get it started, but it wouldn't hit a lick. People passed by and didn't offer to stop and help him, as he tried to push the car. No one seemed to want to show compassion toward him. He had no choice, but to push it off the road, out of the way of traffic. There was a young man, who stopped his vehicle and helped Jim push the car on to a church parking lot. Jim thanked God and then he thanked the young man for helping him in his time of need. Thank God, Jim finally made it home and he was exhausted from his long ordeal.

There is an old saying, 'Whatever goes around comes around", which in essence means that if you do a good deed for someone else, in time the same help will come back to you. I guess it was about 3 weeks later; Jim went to Wal-Mart to get gas for the car. As he pulled away from the gas pumps, he saw a young man trying to push his car off the Wal-Mart parking lot. The same thing was happening to the young man, that had happened to Jim three weeks earlier. No one cared enough to stop to help the young man. Jim stopped to see if the man needed any help, even though he didn't know who he was. He glanced over at the young man and to his surprise it was the same person who had helped him three weeks earlier. Jim told me, after they had finished pushing the man's vehicle to a safe spot, he and the young man laughed about how both of them were at the same time and the same place to help each other. This man showed compassion and in return Jim gave back compassion to the young man. Only God could have worked this out for the both of them. We want our walk with God to be one of compassion and love for our fellowman.

As Christians, we are to follow the example of our Savior, Jesus Christ, and show compassion to others. Sometimes we find it difficult to show compassion for all people. It is easy to show compassion for certain people, but everyone has people in their lives, for whom they struggle to show compassion. I encourage you to pray, that God will convict your heart to have compassion for all people. "That there should be no division in the body, but that the members should have the same care for one another. And if one member suffers, all the members suffer with it; if one member is honored, all the members rejoice with it." (1 Corinthians 12:25-26)

As I said before, it has been over a year since Jim has had a job. At the first of the month we do O.K. but toward the last of the month, money seems to run out and our food supply gets very low. Because of this Jim had to resort to visiting different churches in order to receive food from their food pantries. This has given, both Jim and me a new perspective on those people, who have to beg for food or go through garbage cans to find a meal for that day. We never stopped to think, that without the blessings of God in our lives, we could have been that man or woman digging in the trash can for food. We never want to make the mistake of degrading the homeless or those who have to beg for food, but instead we want to have a compassionate heart for those less fortunate than us. We never thought this could happen to us but it did. Our new motto is "Love is not love until you give it away and we got a lot of love to give."

When we go through trials and troubles, God teaches us how to handle problems, so that we then have the knowledge and sympathetic compassion to help others. As we see their problems, we remember how we felt and how we were able to make it through our difficult times. This, then opens the door to winning souls for the Kingdom of God, because He can use our pain to minister healing into the lives of other people. We become the laborers of God, harvesting souls for His Kingdom. If we are failing to see people as God does, it is because we haven't yet learned to develop godly compassion. Jesus had compassion for those weak in faith and yet, He still reached out to save them. He fed the five thousand by taking care of their physical needs first and then their spiritual needs. First, find a way to reach other's needs and then you will be able to reach their hearts.

"The most important thing in life is to learn how to give out love, and to let it come in."

Chapter 11

Dealing With Negative Emotions

Have you ever felt as if you were alone on a deserted island, with no one around? Have you ever felt as though God had forsaken you? There were times, Jim and I felt so alone, no one cared and God had forsaken us. We called out to God but it seemed He wasn't there. Well, if you are feeling alone and forsaken, take heart, you are not. In fact, many Christians feel the same way right now and even Jesus felt that way too. In Matthew 27:46, Jesus had reached His lowest point in His life. He asked His Father if He had forsaken Him. Jesus cried with a loud voice, Eli, Eli, lama sa bach than ru. This means My God, My God, why hast thou forsaken Me

During these times, when we feel alone, the truth is we are not. God is always with us, to help you, if we will let Him. Be strong and of good courage, do not fear nor be afraid of them; for the Lord, your God, He is the One who goes with you. He will never leave you nor forsake you. (Deuteronomy 31:6). During our difficult times, we experienced many negative emotions, such as hurt, betrayal, anxiety, depression, bitterness, hopelessness and dissatisfaction.

FEELING OF HURT AND BETRAYAL: Have you ever had a person close to you do or say something to hurt you? Betrayal is a hurt, which comes in many forms—a broken promise, a confidence violated, a boundary crossed or a lie exposed. Being hurt by anyone is painful and sometimes this kind of hurt is hard to get over. When someone we love and trust hurts us, the pain seems more intense, because it takes us by surprise. We are hurt, when we least expect it, by those, whom we rely on to be at our side. Betrayal signifies loss: loss of safety, loss of predictability and maybe even loss of a relationship. There comes a time in our lives, when we need to forgive the one who hurt and betrayed us.

FEELING OF ANXIOUSNESS: This means we are not trusting God to take care of us. No matter what problems we have in our lives, Jesus has overcome them. In the world, you will have tribulation, but be of cheer I (Jesus) have over come the world (John 16:33). God says we should not be anxiousness about anything, because He will take care of it all. When we are anxious, it means we are not trusting God to take care of us. He will prove His faithfulness, if we run to Him. Do not seek what you should eat or what you should drink, nor have an anxious mind. For all these things the nations of the world seek after, and your Father knows all these things shall be added unto you. (Luke 12:29-31) God says we don't need to be anxious about anything; we just need to pray about everything.

FEELING OF DEPRESSION: (a down and out feeling): Yes, it is easy for depression to set in. One thing happens after another, with no positive results, which causes you to really get down in your spirit. During our times of trials, depression hit both, Jim and me, leaving us with the feeling of giving up. We had no one to turn to for help and it seemed our prayers were bouncing off the ceiling and falling to the ground. God does not want us to be like that, in fact, He wants us to have the joy of the Lord to raise up in us and chase away the spirit of heaviness. Neither be ye sorry: for the joy of the Lord is your strength. (Nehemiah 8:10)

FEELING OF HOPELESSNESS: Hopelessness is a slow killer, which can soon affect your mind, body and soul. I believed in God, but there were times my flesh would rise up. I am not saying my faith had not gotten weaker, because it had. My physical eyes did not see the good things happening, but instead they saw things getting worst. When I felt my flesh rise up, I would run to God for help. When we choose to put our hope in God, He will meet all our needs and take hopelessness away. No matter how bad things get in our lives, we can always place our hope in God. Now faith is the substance of things hope for, the evidence of things not seen. (Hebrews 12:1)

FEELING OF FEAR: When the devil puts a feeling of fear in us, it takes our mind off of God. Fear wears us down, by worrying about things, which may or may not happen. God does not want us to live in fear! Do whatever you can to stay close to God. When experiencing trials and tribulations, I thought, about the good things of God to try to get my mind off of my troubles. (Philippians 4:8) Finally, brethren, whatsoever things are true, whatsoever things are honest, whatsoever things are just, whatsoever things are pure, whatsoever things are lovely, whatsoever things are of good report; if there be any virtue, and if there be any praise, think on these things. I love to work with the computer and music, so I would keep my mind busy doing the things I love to do. Filling my mind with good thoughts caused fear to soon disappear. For God hasn't given us a spirit of fear but of power and of love and of a sound mind. (2 Timothy 1:7)

FEELING OF BEING DISSATISFIED: It is easy to focus on the negative and look for everything wrong in our lives. When we have constant unrest in our lives, because everything around us seems miserable, we develop an attitude of wanting things to be so much different, that we sacrifice our peace. Whenever we feel discouraged by our circumstances, remember that the apostle Paul said, I have learned abased and I have learned both to be full and to be hungry, both to abound and to suffer need, I can do all things through Christ who strengthens me. (Philippians 4:11-13) It is possible to find contentment, rest, peace and joy in any situation.

FEELING OF BITTERNESS AND ANGER: We are responsible for what we do, say, think, and feel. Nobody can cause us to be bitter. We choose, whether or not to respond to situations in a bitter way. Naturally we can get rid of all bitterness, resentment, rage and anger, brawling and slander, along with every form of malice, if we wish to do so. What makes us bitter is our attitude toward people and circumstances. It's not the people or the circumstances, but it is the enemy's influence on them. Some people are bitter, because they refuse to let go by forgiving themselves. They often trap themselves in bitter bargaining.

THE FEELING OF RESENTMENT: Resentment is another form of anger. When you are hurt or when you are fearful and threatened of your security, then anger is the result. If you don't deal properly with anger and allow it to continue in your life, then it becomes resentment. If you don't make it an ally, rather than a detriment, you will continue holding on to it. Resentment is keeping score on people, who have hurt you, with the intention some day of getting even. If you never release the hurt, they did to you; it will eat you alive spiritually. Resentment is the great destroyer of relationships.

Why should we be anxious, angry, depressed, bitter, hopeless, dissatisfied or fearful? We all have or will experience these emotions in our lives. Do not feel bad about having them but don't live with them either! God will give us strength and understanding to resist them. In our distress, we can call on God and He will hear us. If we stop to see and try to understand the different possibilities for our suffering, it will help us overcome our pain and cause our faith to grow in the midst of it.

Chapter 12

Dealing With Negative Thoughts

It is easy to let our minds get out of control. There were times we let our minds think about all the negative things that were happening. We knew it was the devil trying to get our minds off of God and the good things He was preparing for us. The devil was trying to make us give up. We realized we should have caught his lies the minute they entered our minds, but instead we entertained them. The devil is a clever deceiver who will come to each one of us and try to speak lies into our minds. We have to be on guard 24-7.

Do you ever have certain thoughts that play over and over in your mind like an old broken record? Has the thought "what if" ever entered your mind such as "What if" I had done things differently than I did" or "What if" I just ended it all?" Have you ever had "if only" thoughts such as "If only I hadn't done that' or "If only I had been there?" Do you ever have self-punishing thoughts such as "No one cares about me,' "I am no good" or "nothing I do ever turns out right." If you have had thoughts like these, please know IT IS NOT GOD!! It is the devil trying to gain control of your mind.

Life has much suffering, but often we suffer unnecessarily, because of lies we believe about our circumstances and ourselves. We accept the fact that the words that are spoken to our souls by the devil are the truth. We can become fearful, depressed, lonely, angry, confused, insecure, hopeless, beaten-down, worried and full of self-pity, all because of lies we believed. We can overcome each of these lies with prayer, faith and the truth of God's Word.

We must be aware that the devil is trying to steal God's Word from us, because he knows there is power in God's Words. He will do whatever he can to get us to question God and His Word. When thoughts that you think begin to make you question God, BEWARE! you are being set up by the devil. Remember there is a way that seems right to a man, but its end is the way of death. (Proverbs 14:12) Certain thoughts may appear to you to be so real, but when you hold them next to God's Word, the lie is exposed.

The devil's deception is his on going plan to attack. Jesus said the devil was a murderer from the beginning and does not stand in the truth, because there is no truth in him. When he speaks a lie, he speaks from his own resources, for he is a liar and the father of it. (John 8:44) The only power the devil has is in getting us to believe his lies. If we don't believe his lies, he is powerless to get his work done.

Refusing to entertain negative thoughts in our mind is part of resisting the devil. We don't have to live with confusion or mental oppression. We don't have to walk as the rest of the Gentiles walk, in the futility of their minds, having their understanding darkened, being alienated from the life of God, because of the ignorance that is in them, and the hardening of their hearts. (Ephesians 4:17-18) Instead we can have clarity and knowledge: even though the devil tries to convince us that our future is as hopeless as his or that we are failures with no purpose, values, gifts or abilities. God says exactly the opposite of what the devil tells us. Believe God and don't listen to anything else!

When you learn to transform every negative event of your life into a positive one you'll stop being a prisoner of your past and become a designer of your future.

Chapter 13

Sowing Good or Bad Seeds

Holy Father, It is Your Holy Spirit who lives in us and who enables us to grow in our love for You, our Joy in Jesus; our Peace in the midst of this world; Long-suffering when we are struck on every side; Goodness in the midst of the devil tempting us to do bad things; Faith rather than fear or doubt or unbelief; Meekness so that we depend upon You: Temperance so we are balanced in our lives.

We believe today, that we have faith to produce these fruits, as Your Spirit works, with our spirit to grow them. Heavenly Father, we are determined, that we are going to grow good fruit of the spirit every day, with your help, guidance, strength and love. Amen.

Whether we realize it or not, in trials and tribulations of our everyday lives, we are planting seeds. The seeds we plant can either be good or bad ones. It is a fact that in due season the seeds we sow each day of our lives are going to bring forth either good or bad fruit in days to come. "But the fruit of the Spirit is love, joy, peace, long-suffering, gentleness, goodness, faith" (Colossians 3:12; Romans 15:14; 1 Corinthians 13:7) "meekness, temperance: against such there is no law." (Galatians 6:10)

The fruit of the Spirit is LOVE. Only if we live in love can we fulfill the will of God in our lives. The believer must become love-driven, love inspired and love mastered (2 Corinthians 5:14). Without the fruit of the Spirit (LOVE), we are just religious noise (1 Corinthians 13:1).

1. Joy is loves strength.

2. Peace is loves security.

3. Long-suffering is loves patience.

4. Gentleness is loves conduct.

5. Goodness is loves character.

6. Faith is loves confidence.

7. Meekness is loves humility.

8. Temperance is loves victory.

Against such there is no law.

There were times we didn't let the love of God shine in us. We have asked God to plant His love in us in such a profound and powerful way, that we are able to fully experience it. We ask God for His love to flow through us to others. Jesus said, "If you keep My commandments, you will abide in My love, just as I have kept My Fathers commandments and abide in His love (John 15:10). We asked God to help us obey all of His commandments, so that His love would blossom in us."

The first of the manifestations of the Spirit is love, which is the key to all the others. Along with temperance (Self-Control) and love is the bookend, which helps hold the other fruit in place. Its divine characteristics are detailed in 1 Corinthians 13. It's a love, which surpasses human understanding and causes a person to be filled, with the fullness of God. (Ephesians 3:18-19) His supernatural love is shed abroad, in our hearts, by the Holy Spirit (Romans 5:5). The spiritual love is not just a feeling or an emotion, but rather it is a decision. The Fruit of the Spirit causes us to make a decision to love even when we don't feel like it.

Paul writes in (Philippians 1:9): And this I pray that your love may abound yet more and more. The word abound means to grow. God wants our love to grow so big, that it will chase people down and overtake them. When we walk in the love of God, everything else will fall into place. A new commandment I give unto you, that ye love one another, as I have loved you, that ye also love one another. By this shall all men know that ye are my disciples, if ye have love one to another. (John 13:34-35)

Love is first for a very good reason, because it was out of love, that God created human beings. He continually reached out to man despite his stubborn ways. It was out of love, that God sacrificed His only Son Jesus, to save man from sin. Today it is out of love, that God sends believers, in Jesus, to spread the Gospel, so that more people will be saved from their sins. The type of love mentioned in Galatians is unconditional. It's the love, which a parent has for their child, which is selfless and sacrificing. This is why love is listed as the first fruit of the Spirit.

Joy is different from happiness in that it is a deep contentment. A person finds joy when accepting the gift of salvation, through Jesus Christ. If a person bears the fruit of joy, this allows this same joy to spread to others and causes people to praise God and thank Him for all of His blessings. Joy is the fruit of the Spirit, that keeps a person going, even when they feel persecuted and can even sustain their life.

God is truly a God of peace, because He longed for peace between Himself and man. He grants people peace, through His Son Jesus, who is often referred to as the Prince of Peace. People can spread this fruit of the Spirit by keeping peace in situations. After all, Jesus said in the beatitudes that blessed are the peacemakers.

Long-suffering or patience helps people to be better Christians and human beings. Sometimes, when people call upon God in prayer, His answer doesn't always come in earthly time. Enduring the struggle, until God finally answers, is a great example of patience and trust.

Gentleness comes right along with patience. Gentleness doesn't necessarily mean timid. Jesus was gentle, but not at all timid, about the Truth. Each Christian should follow the example of Jesus.

Goodness or kindness is so simple, yet so difficult for many people to attain. Goodness often keeps people from making careless mistakes, after all, people are representatives of Jesus and goodness must be evident in each person.

Faith, in Jesus, helps people to abandon the desire to do bad things. Like a plant that is cultivated and cared for, a Christians faith can bare the Fruits of the Holy Spirit. It is not so difficult for you to bare these fruits, if you take the time to pray, read Gods Word, surround yourself with fellow believers, worship regularly and commit to tithing. By doing this, believers will not only see more good in others, but he or she will see their own relationship, with God grow stronger.

Jesus said in the beatitudes, that the meek shall inherit the earth. A good example of meekness is when a person can turn the other cheek, when faced with a confrontational situation in their lives. Sometimes people want to fight back, but with the Holy Spirit each person will find, that meekness is a valuable way to spread the Gospel. Even Jesus had His meek moments, such as, when the soldiers took Him away, from the Garden of Gethsemane. Another great example of meekness was, when He displayed great temperance or self-control, by resisting the temptation of the devil in the desert. With the fruit of the Holy Spirit, within a person, it is easier to resist temptation and maintain temperance. Self-control is an important fruit, because:

GOD IS WATCHING!!!!!!!!!!!!!!!!!

It is just as easy to sow bad seeds, as it is good ones. Sometimes we don't realize, that we are sowing these bad seeds, until it is too late. We call ourselves Christians (Christ-like), but yet some have hate, deceit, spitefulness, jealousy, envy, and strife in their hearts. For where envying and strife is, there is confusion and every evil work. (James 3:16) Why do we sow seeds of pride, boastfulness, backbiting, malignity and disobedience among brothers and sisters in Jesus? Do we take time to look into our hearts and see what is in there? I can understand these bad seeds being sown, among the sinners, but the biggest thing that bothers me is the fact, that this is happening, among the Christians. We are called by God to uplift and encourage our fellowman and woman, but instead we find ways to tear them down. We say we love God, but at the same time we have hatred, in our hearts, for our brothers and sisters. If a man says, I love God and hates his brother, he is a liar: for he that loveth not his brother whom he hath seen, how can he love God whom he hath not seen. (1 John 4:20) There are a few bad seeds that we sometimes sow that God hates.

In Proverbs 6:16-19, it tells of seven deadly sins:

1. A proud look
2. A lying tongue
3. Hands that shed innocent blood
4. A heart that devises wicked imaginations
5 Feet that are swift in running to mischief
6. A false witness speaking things that are not true
7. A person who sows discord among the brothers or sisters.

Truthfully, we have been guilty of sowing a few of these bad seed in the past, but we are trying to do better. This past year, God has shown us a lot of things we needed to change within ourselves. There were times we didn't let the love of God shine in us. We have asked God to plant His love in us, in such a profound and powerful way, that we are able to fully experience it. We asked God also, that His love would flow through us to others. We asked God to help us obey all of His laws, so that nothing will keep the fullness of His love from blossoming in us.

Chapter 14

Why Do We Go Through Trials

God allows trials and tribulation to come along into our lives, with the purpose of helping us grow in Him. God gives us strength, through His Holy Spirit to overcome those trials. All we have to do is put our trust in Him and let Him bring us through them. Some Christians fail as they try to go through their own hardships, because they do not understand that they need to trust God. Every time they try to go through a trial on their own strength, they fall! Here are a few of the reasons we go through trials:

1. Trials and tribulation happen to us so that the glory and power of God can be revealed in and through us. We may not understand, at the time, why certain things are happening and we may never know, why we have to go through them. God's glory will be revealed in us, when we turn to God, in the midst, of our difficult situations.

2. God uses trials and tribulation to purify us. The Bible tells us in 1 Peter 4:1 that Jesus suffered for us in the flesh and we will suffer too. Our suffering, in difficult times, will burn sin and

selfishness out of our lives. God allows these times of suffering, so we will learn to live for Him and not for ourselves. We need to pursue His Will and not our own will. In Hebrews 12:10, God desires us to be partakers of His holiness. He wants us to let go of worldly things and cling to what is most important in life-HIM!

3. God uses our trials and tribulations to discipline us. Do not despise the chastening of the Lord nor be discouraged when he rebukes you: for whom the Lord loves He chastens and scourges every son whom He receives. (Hebrews 12:5-6) There are times, when Jim and I got to big for our britches and God had to take us down a notch. We thought we could handle our problems by ourselves, so we didn't let God work them out.

Every time a person rises above their trials and finds the joy, love, peace and the light of Jesus, their faith will increase. God will meet them in the midst of their trials and He will not only purify them, but will increase their compassion for the suffering of others. God and His glory will be revealed in each individual, who continues to live for Him.

Even though Jim and I are in the midst of a trial it will soon be over and happiness will be on its way. For his anger endureth but for a moment, in

His favour is life: weeping may endure for the night, but joy cometh in the morning. (Psalm 30:5)

God, grant me the serenity to accept the things I can't change; the courage to change the things I can; and the wisdom to know the difference

Chapter 15

Trials And Tribulations
Who is Responsible? God or The Devil

Picture yourself standing there, with God on your right side. GOD IS A GOOD GOD! He is the Creator, Father, Judge, Defender, Preserver, Shepherd, Healer, Counselor, and Provider, Shelter in the Storm and Deliverer. He offers abundant life through Jesus, unending blessings, grace, mercy, strength, health, victory, vitality, joy, peace, love, security, contentment, zeal for good works, meekness, humility, gentleness and self-control. He loves you and wants to help you.

Now picture the devil standing there on your left side. THE DEVIL IS EVIL!! He is the father of lies, trespasser, destroyer, murderer, accuser, adversary, condemner and thief. He offers death, destruction, sickness, disease, pain, infirmity, malady, poverty, tragedy, hate, jealousy, depression, defeat, bitterness and doubt. He will tempt, afflict, oppose, sift, beguile and deceive Gods children. He hates and wants to destroy you. The devil, if you let him, will do everything he can to kill, steal and destroy your life. (See John 10:10)

There is an enemy (devil), who opposes all that God is, and everything He stands for. The devil comes against a person, who believes in God or tries to live a godly life. The devil was an original created cherub, a living, loving, breathing instrument, who brought praise to God (Ezekiel 28:12-17). The problem, with recognizing the devil, is we see him as an ugly, hideous, creature with two pointed horns and a pointed tail. This couldn't be further from the truth. The Bible tells us that he can transform himself into an angel of light. (2 Corinthians 11:14) He disguises himself, so that he doesn't look threatening and he lulls us into thinking that we are not in any danger. (2 Corinthians 11:14) The devil is now, in a fallen state, because of greed (lust for more and pride). Jesus said unto them, I beheld satan fallen as lightning from Heaven. (Luke 10:18)

If you removed the D from the devils name what do you get? The answer is EVIL, which describes the very essence of his being. He hates God and what He stands for. We become the enemy of the devil, when we come to God. The devil knows he can't destroy God, but he can destroy God's children, the closest and dearest thing to Him! IF WE LET HIM!!!!!!!

Just as God has a plan for us, so does the devil. The devil's plan is to steal from us and destroy our lives. He never stops in what he is doing, nor does he take a day off. The devil is constantly trying to find ways to see, that his plan for our lives is fulfilled. 1 Peter 5:8-11 says we need to be sober and vigilant, because our adversary the devil is like a roaring lion walking about, seeking, whom he may devour. The devil is roaring to get our attention, so that we get our minds off of God. He knows, when we get our minds off of God, he can slowly come in to destroy us. Yes, we can rise up against his roar. Yes, we can resist him, because our God of grace and mercy establishes us in maturity and molds us firmly in His image. Submit yourselves therefore to God. Resist the devil, and he will flee from you. (James 4:8)

Most of the time we're able to recognize the attacks of the devil. We have to keep our guard up 24-7 or if we don't, he will slip in and get us off track. 99% of the time he puts thoughts in our minds, that don't need to be there. For example, he will attempt to make us believe, that we deserve every bad thing, which happens to us. Deserving is not the issue with God. We didn't deserve to have Gods precious Son, Jesus die for us, yet He loved us enough He was willing to shed His blood on Calvary. We need to ask God to help us discern the devil's works in our lives

Many people have asked this question, "I'm a good person so why is the devil attacking me?" He attacks anyone, who loves God and lives for Him. We are his targets, as long as we have the heart for the things of God. The greater our commitment is to God the more the devil will try to harass us. He will do all he can to wear us down, with discouragement, sickness, confusion, guilt, strife, fear, depression and defeat. He will try to threaten our minds, emotions, health, work, family and relationships. He will try to blind us, to the truth and get us to believe his lies. The truth is:

The Devil Has Lost.

Jesus Is Still No. 1

My friend, at some point in your life, you will have to make a critical decision whether or not to follow God or the devil. God says that you cannot have two masters. No man can serve two masters: for either he will hate the one, and love the other; or else he will hold to the one, and despise the other. Ye cannot serve God and mammon. (Matthew 6:24)

There is a conflict going on inside of you. One is fighting for "EVIL." He is full of anger, envy, sorrow, regret, greed, arrogance, self-pity, guilt, resentment, inferiority, lies, false pride, superiority, self-doubt, and ego. "The other is fighting for "GOOD." He is full of joy, peace, love, hope, serenity, humility, kindness, benevolence, empathy, generosity, truth, compassion, and faith."

You will ask the question, "Which one will win?" The answer is: THE ONE YOU FEED THE MOST. Think about it, my friend!

Chapter 16

Spiritual Warfare

Spiritual warfare is a all out war between the forces of God and the forces of anti-christ, led by one of God's created angelic being named Lucifer. He is more commonly known to us as satan or the devil. Satan is derived, from the Hebrew word, meaning opponent. The word devil, in the Greek, is translated accuser or slanderer. His main objective, as it is related to mankind, is to accuse God's people as he did in the book of Job. Whenever God's children stumble and fall, or sin against God, satan accuses them before God's throne.

There are two important things we must understand about satan, which will help us deal with his wiles.

(1) His pride and arrogance makes him think he can really be like God.

(2) He has an intense jealousy and hatred for mankind because of the great love and the plan of salvation, which has been offered to mankind, but not to fallen angels. Jesus Christ made all this possible when He stole the keys of death, hell and the grave from the devil.

"For though we live in this world, we do not wage war as the world does. The weapons we fight with are not the weapons of the world. On the contrary, they have divine power to demolish strongholds. We demolish arguments and every pretension that sets itself up against the knowledge of God, and we take captive every thought to make it obedient to Christ." (2 Corinthians 1:3-5)

Spiritual warfare is a reality of the Christian life, but remember, although we may lose some battles, we have the final victory! Since the devil has nothing to lose, he will take as many people as he can down his path of mass destruction. When the devil succeeds in doing this, God hurts, like a parent does over losing a child. This sort of hatred is very much in keeping with the devil's character. Satan is a leech; he is so lacking in life, that the only life he has left is, what he can suck out of the living.

The very first thing you will need to know is that satan, his demons, and all of their supernatural powers have been totally defeated by Jesus, when He died on the cross and rose the third day, for all of our sins. Here are extremely, powerful verses that you will need to have underneath your belt, if you are ever forced to deal with any kind of a direct, demonic attack either against yourself or anyone else you may know. Demons hate, and I mean hate, every single one of these verses, as they are all a constant reminder to the fact, that Satan and his army of demons are all defeated. These verses also remind satan, that he has no chance against any true, born-again Christian, who knows who they really are in JESUS CHRIST, how to wield the Sword of the Holy Spirit, and how to walk, with the anointing, that God has given them.

1. Through death He might destroy him who had the power of death, that is, the devil, and release those who through fear of death were all their lifetime subject to bondage. (Hebrews 2:14)
2. He has delivered us from the power of darkness and translated us into the kingdom of the Son of His love, in whom we have redemption through His blood, the forgiveness of sins. (Colossians 1:13)
3. Having disarmed principalities and powers, He made a public spectacle of them, triumphing over them in it. (Colossians 2:15)
4. And they overcame him by the blood of the Lamb and by the word of their testimony, and they did not love their lives to the death. (Revelation 12:11)
5. Let this mind be in you which was also in Christ Jesus, who, being in the form of God, did not consider it robbery to be equal with God, but made Himself of no reputation, taking the form of a servant, and coming in like the likeness of men. And being found in appearance as a man, He humbled Himself and became obedient to the point of death, even the death of the cross.
6. Therefore God has also highly exalted Him and given Him the name which is above every name,

that at the name of Jesus every knee should bow, of those in heaven and of those on earth, and those under the earth, and that every tongue shall confess that Jesus Christ is Lord, to the glory of God the Father. (Philippians 2:5-11)

7. Ye are of God, little children, and have overcome them: because greater is he that is in you, than he that is in the world. (1 John 4:4)

8. Be sober, be vigilant; because your adversary the devil, as a roaring lion, walketh about, seeking whom he may devour: Whom resist steadfast in the faith. (1 Peter 5:8,9)

We are in a war against sin and worldly desires. Take the armor of God, the shield of faith and the sword of the living God and Fight!!!

The Armor of God

Be strong in the Lord and in the power of His might. Put on the whole armor of God that you may be able to stand against the wiles of the devil. For we do not wrestle against flesh and blood, but against principalities, against powers, against the rulers of the darkness of this age, against spiritual hosts of wickedness in the heavenly places. Therefore take up the whole armor of God, that you may be able to withstand in the evil day, and having done all, to stand. Stand therefore, having girded your waist with truth, having put on the breastplate of righteousness, and having shod your feet with the preparation of the gospel of peace; above all, taking the shield of faith with which you will be able to quench all the fiery darts of the wicked one." And take the helmet of salvation, and the sword of the Spirit, which is the word of God; praying always with all prayer and supplication in the Spirit, being watchful to this end with all perseverance and supplication for all the saints . . ." (Ephesians 6:10-18)

God's armor brings victory because it is far more, than a protective covering. It is the very life of Jesus Christ Himself. Put on the armor of light, wrote Paul in his letter to the Romans, clothe yourselves with the Lord Jesus Christ. (Romans 13:12-14) When you do, He becomes your hiding place, and shelter in the storm, just as He was to David. Hidden in Him, you can count on His victory, for He not only covers you as a shield, He also fills you with His life.

Belt of TRUTH

Know The Truth

Stand therefore having your loins girt about with truth."
—Ephesians 6:14-

"Wherefore gird up the loins of your mind, be sober, and hope to the end for the grace that is to be brought unto you at the revelation of JesusChrist."
—I Peter 1:13-

We need to "provide for honest things not only in the sight of the Lord, but also in the sight of men."
—2 Corinthians 8:21-

Yes, we need to be truthful concerning all things; but we also need to stand on the "truth" of the Bible. When we face trials and tribulations, we need to "tighten" our belt, while standing on truths written in the Word of God. What we know in the good times, we need to hang on to in the troublesome times. We might just end up tightening our belt a notch or two. However, the good news is that "God is faithful, who will not suffer you to be tempted (whether it be doubting or giving up) above that ye are able; but will with the temptation also make a way to escape, that ye may be able to bear it." (I Corinthians 10:13)

Thank You, Jesus, for showing me the truth about yourself and especially about myself. Thank You for reminding me that You are the only God, the Creator of Heaven and earth, the King of the universe, my Father who loves me, and my Shepherd who leads me. You are my wisdom, my counselor, my hope, and my strength. You are everything I need each day.

Breastplate of RIGHTEOUSNESS

Righteousness of Jesus In You

"Stand therefore having your loins girt about with truth, and having on the breastplate of righteousness."—Ephesians 6:14—

"But let us, who are of the day, be sober, putting on the breastplate of faith and love; and for an helmet, the hope of salvation."—I Thessalonians 5:8-

Whenever the enemy tries to bring up your past to accuse you, the breastplate of righteousness is your trusty defense. If the Spirit of Christ dwells in you, then God receives you as His son or daughter, no matter what the devil says. "For he [God] hath made him [Jesus] to be sin for us, who knew no sin; that we might be made the righteousness of God in him." (II Corinthians 5:21) The righteousness of Christ in you is what matters not your shortcomings and failures.

Thank You Jesus, for showing me the truth about myself-that on my own, I could never be good enough to live in Your presence. Thank You for taking my sins to the cross and offering me Your righteous life. JESUS, show me any sin, that I need to confess right now, so that nothing will hinder me from being filled with Your overflowing Spirit (take time for confession). Thank You for forgiving me and for filling me with Your righteous life.

Shield of FAITH

Living By Faith

"Above all, taking the shield of faith, wherewith ye shall be able to quench all the fiery darts of the wicked."—Ephesians 6:16-

"But let us, who are of the day, be sober, putting on the breastplate of faith and love; and for an helmet, the hope of salvation."—I Thessalonians 5:8-

In Romans 10:17 Paul writes: "Faith comes by hearing and hearing by the Word of God." Thus we increase our faith by reading the Bible. Faith works in love (Galatians 5:6) and "perfect love casteth out all fear."(I John 1:18) Therefore, Faith (Forsaking All In Trusting Him) casts out fear (False Evidence Appearing Real). Thus if you want to live a life, without fear you need to read, study, and meditate on the Word of God.

Thank You, Jesus, for helping me have faith in You. I choose to count on what You have shown me about yourself and everything you have promised me in your Word.

Sandals of PEACE

Inner Peace And Readiness

"And your feet shod with the preparation of the gospel of peace."—Ephesians 6:14-

"How beautiful are the feet of them that preach the gospel of peace, and bring glad tidings of good things!"—Romans 10:15-

We need to "preach the word and be instant in season and out of season" (II Timothy 4:2) and we must be obedient to the Lord's command in Mark 16:15 to "Go ye into all the world, and preach the gospel to every creature." Yet we are sent forth "as sheep in the midst of wolves; so we must be wise as serpents and harmless as doves." (Matthew 10:16)

Thank You, Jesus for helping me have faith in You.

Helmet of SALVATION

The Hope of Salvation

And take the helmet of salvation, and the sword of the Spirit, which is the Word of God."—Ephesians 6:17-

"For he put on righteousness as a breastplate, and an helmet of salvation upon his head."
—Isaiah 59:17-

And take the helmet of salvation, and the sword of the Spirit, which is the Word of God."
—Ephesians 6:17-

The helmet of salvation guards our minds, for the battle against the enemy is in the mind. The helmet of salvation also assures us of two things: (1) We will have eternal life in Heaven (2) God has a special plan for us.

Thank You, Jesus for promising me salvation both for today's battles and for all eternity.

Sword of the Spirit

The Word of God

Hebrews 4:12; Matthew 4:2-11; 1 Peter 3:15; Psalm 119:110-112

"And take the helmet of salvation, and the sword of the Spirit, which is the Word of God."
—Ephesians 6:17-

The Sword of the Spirit is the Word of God breathed from our spirits and released from our mouths, mingled with and energized by the breath or Spirit of God, causing it to be filled with His divine life and ability.

"Praying always with all prayer and supplication in the Spirit, and watching thereunto with all perseverance and supplication for all saints."—Ephesians 6:18-

"Be careful for nothing; but in everything by prayer and supplication with thanksgiving, let your requests be made known unto God."—Philippians 4:6-

"Pray without ceasing."—I Thessalonians 5:17-

For the weapons of our warfare are not carnal, but mighty through God to the pulling down of strongholds;)—II Corinthians 10:4-

My friend put on the whole armor of God so that you can fight the good fight of faith!!

Chapter 17

How To Fight The Devil

The following is compiled from the writings of the late David Brandt Berg. (1919-1994)

Once we are "born again" (John 3:3), we not only find a wonderful new life of love, peace and happiness, we also find ourselves in a WAR!—A war of the Worlds between the World of evil and the Kingdom of God!

In the old World War I trench warfare, it wasn't until you came out of your trench and started attacking the enemy's territory, that he would really open up and let you have it, with all of his big guns! Now that you're saved, as far as the Devil is concerned, you have "gone over the top", and he will do all he can to oppose and stop you! You are now a Christian soldier in God's Army, and a potential threat to hundreds of thousands of others of the devil's captives! He knows that you now belong to JESUS forever and that he can never get you back, so since he can't stop you from being a Christian, the next best thing he tries to do is to try to stop you, from being an active Christian. He tries to make you a dead (unproductive) Christian, instead of a real live (protective) one! He'll fight and try to stop you, from serving the Lord, and keep you, from being a good example to win others, because he's afraid, that he might lose others from his clutches because of you!

Once we are born again," we not only find a wonderful new way of life, peace and happiness, but we also find ourselves in a war. This war of the worlds, between the world of evil (satan's kingdom) and the Kingdom of God!

God Is In Control

God's Word says, "We are not ignorant of Satan's devices" (2 Corinthians 2:11) We should beware of the Devil's devices and be on guard against the "fiery darts" (Ephesians 6:16) of discouragement, pride, fear, jealousy, selfishness, doubts, negative thoughts etc., that he fires at us to try to hinder us! But the enemy can't lay a finger on us, unless the Lord allows him to!—And if the Lord does allow him to, it's only for our good, to make us stronger fighters, to teach us lessons or to draw us closer to Jesus!

Always remember, that as a Christian, you have nothing to fear from the devil or his forces, because JESUS is with you! In fact, you have power over all the devils of Hell, including Satan himself! God's Word tells us; "Greater is He (JESUS) that is in you, than he (the devil) that is in the World!"(1

John 4:4) Jesus also said, "All power is given unto me in Heaven and in Earth!"(Matthew 28:18) And you have JESUS and all of His power! He says, "Behold, I give unto you power over ALL the power of the devil!"(Luke 10:19) So through the power of prayer, in JESUS' name, you say to your enemy, Get thee behind me Satan and leave me alone! When he tries to hinder you, with negative or discouraging thoughts, through the power of prayer, you can command him to flee and he has no choice, but to do so. James 4:7

Don't Let The Devil Get You Down!

One of the devil's favorite tools, to use on Christians, is discouragement! He tries to get you looking, at your own mistakes, sins, weaknesses and failures! He just picks and picks, at all your little flaws and shortcomings and exaggerates and blows them out of proportion! This is one of the devil's favorite tactics. He knows, that it's impossible for him to defeat you, as long as you keep on fighting, so he tries to persuade you, that you're a hopeless case and you might as well surrender and give up.

What is discouragement? It is a loss of courage resulting from a lack of Faith. "Faith comes from hearing the Word of God" (Romans 10:17), so when you feel discouraged, the quickest remedy is to start praying, quoting scriptures, reading the Word and telling the devil he's a liar! (John 8:44) You have to fight discouragement with prayer and the Word! Then your faith will grow, the doubts will flee, and you'll be on the road to victory!

How To Resist Temptations

A temptation is the thought or desire to do wrong. Nobody can keep temptations from coming, but you don't have to yield to them! As the wise old saying goes, "You can't keep the birds from flying over your head, but you can keep them from building a nest in your hair!" In other words, you can't keep the devil, from saying things to you and tempting you with his bad thoughts, but you can keep from yielding to him!

A lot of people condemn themselves and feel bad and wicked, because they've thought or been tempted with sinful thoughts, but even JESUS was tempted, in all points, the same as we are! (Hebrews 4:15; Matthew 4:1-10) It's no sin when the devil tempts you to do something. Sin is brought about, when you yield to temptation. The way to resist and get rid of temptations and negative thoughts is to read your Bible. Pray, think about good, faith building and encouraging thoughts, instead of entertaining the thoughts of the devil. "Whatsoever things are true, honest, just, pure, lovely and good, think on these things!"(Philippians 4:8) Isaiah says, "Thou wilt keep him in perfect peace whose mind is stayed on Thee, because he trusteth in Thee."(Isaiah 26:3) If you keep your mind on JESUS, you won't have time to think about the distracting lies of the enemy!

Praise Power!

The best defense is an offense, and if you really want to get the devil on the run, just start praising the Lord! Count your blessings and thank and praise Jesus for all, which He has done for you! The power of positive praise is just terrific and really puts the devil on the run! Chase the devil and his darkness away by simply letting the Light in! The enemy hates songs of prayer and praise to Jesus, and he especially hates our positive, active service for the Lord! So don't just sit there, do something positive! Resist, defy and attack the enemy by taking positive action and doing something good! Go on the attack and THINK positively, TALK positively, SING positively, PRAY positively and ACT positively!

Sock It To Him With The Word!

When the enemy is attacking you, don't just stand there and take it. Hit him back!!! Quote scriptures and sock it to him with the Word! That's the way JESUS fought back when the devil tempted and lied to Him! He just quoted Scriptures: "It is written!" He fought him with the Word! (Matthew 4:1-11) When it comes to fighting the devil, God's Words are almost like spiritual bullets or death rays, and they just blast him! Every word absolutely zaps him! In the Bible's description of a Christian soldier's armor, the one offensive weapon described is "the sword of the Spirit, which is the Word of God"! (Ephesians 6:17) In fact, it is "quick (alive) and powerful, and sharper than any two-edged sword!"(Hebrews 4:12) The Word is the most powerful thing you can use! The enemy can't take the Word! He'll turn tail & run! So the next time he raises his ugly head & tries to tempt, hinder or slow you down, pull out the white-hot sword of the Spirit, the Word of God, and cut the Devil to the heart!

Memorize Scriptures To Resist The Devil!

Often the only weapons you have immediately on hand, with which, to fight the enemy are the Scriptures that you've memorized. This is why it's so important to memorize and fill your mind and heart with positive, encouraging, strengthening and faith-building thoughts, from God's Word. The most effective way, with which to fight the enemy is to memorize those scriptures, which you can continually quote to yourself and even to the devil, when he attacks you! Fill your mind with the Light of God's Word, and the darkness will flee! Quote Scriptures and really rebuke the devil and declare your faith and trust in the Lord and His Word by even quoting it out loud! Drown his lies out! Just shout! Don't doubt! Kick him out!

Ask For Prayer!

Sometimes we really need help from our brothers and sisters to fight the battle together against the enemy! "One can chase a thousand, but two can put ten thousand to flight!" (Deuteronomy 32:30), and it is often a great help to have someone else pray with you, when you feel oppressed, distressed or attacked by the enemy! Jesus said, "Where two or three of you are gathered together in My Name, there am I in the midst of them!"(Matthew 18:20) There is great power in united prayer!

Fight The Good Fight!

The best way to stop an attack is to counter-attack! The best defense is an offense! Fight the Devil positively! Attack, attack, attack! The Bible says to "Draw nigh unto God, resist the enemy and he will flee from you"! (James 4:7) We can't just be passive and expect God to do it all! We have to be good fighters and resist the enemy! We have to wage a spiritual militant warfare against him!

The only way the devil can defeat you is if you surrender! So KEEP FIGHTING and you can't lose! Keep wielding the weapon of the Word and you'll win! Keep on holding on to God's promises!—Don't let go! Keep on going for Jesus!—Don't stop! Keep on keeping on!

May God help you to be fighters who like to fight for the Lord with the weapon of his Word, who enjoy defeating the devil!

Chapter 18

From Then Until Now

It has been over 5 years since we started writing our book "ONLY GOD." Jim and I have realized, through our times of testing, that we were not perfect and made many mistakes and misjudged things. We know God was always there with us and that He is still right there, helping us get through our difficult times. So what!!!! We've made mistakes, but we are not going to let the devil beat us down, because of them. With God's help, we are going to keep on trucking in Jesus. Nobody is good enough, smart enough, cute enough or successful enough to be acceptable to a just and holy God. When God looks at us through the eyes of Jesus, we become pleasing in His sight.

We still don't have all the answers, to what has happened to us and chances are we may never know. The answer to the question "Why?" does not seem to be that important anymore. The important things are the lessons we have learned from them all.

We have learned to take one day at a time. God showed us, that our faith lies in the boundaries of today, for tomorrow is but a glimmer of hope. We are trying to stay focused on God, who will keep us in His peace, as He moves us, into the future He has planned for us.

We have learned, that God is able to take nothing and make something out of it. He, out of nothing can create miracles in us and for us! God works in ways we could never conceive. Without God we are nothing and we will never have anything, but with God we are somebody and we have it all.

We have learned from the things, which we have experienced, that God is at work, producing a faith in us, that is being tried and the final outcome will be better than gold. God is working to get us to stop focusing, on the impossible and start believing, that all things are possible through Him. We must stop trying to think our way out of our situations and rely on God to direct our paths. When all else fails and when our every plan and scheme has failed, it is the time for us to give everything to God. No, truthfully, we should give everything to God in the beginning, which would save us a lot of heartache. It is time we put our confidence in God, instead of looking elsewhere. God is urging us to quit focusing on how hopeless we think our situations are and start focusing on all the blessings that He has for us.

We have learned, that if God delays the answer or says no to something, that we have asked in prayer, we can be assured, that He has a very good reason. God has all power and can do anything and nothing is impossible to Him. He has promised to answer every prayer, prayed in the name of Jesus, but only according to His Divine Will. We must all ask in full assurance of faith, expecting an answer from God.

We have learned, that there are two important priorities in our lives. Our first priority is to love God, with all our heart and soul. Our second priority is to show God's love to our family, friends and neighbors. "And ye shall love the Lord, your God with all your heart, with all your soul and with all your strength. This is the first commandment. And the second is like unto the first, that ye shall love your neighbor as yourself. There is no other commandment greater than these." (Mark 12:30-31)

Who is the source of love in this world? It certainly is not the devil! It is God!!! In 1 John 4:5,12, John tells us that God is love. His love is manifested toward us in the form of His own Son, Jesus. Jesus dying, for us, is the love of God in action. Therefore, when we have God, who is love, we should love others. If we say we are of God and do not love others, we are liars. Love is a sure sign that God lives in our hearts. People can see God, when they see His children loving one another. Love causes people to say. "That person lets me know there is a God, because He is a God of Love."

Where Love Is, There God Is,

For God Is Love.

As Jim and I sit here thinking about the events of the last five years particularly, the last two, we realize we could not have made it without God. We have remained faithful to God, through all our trials, tribulations, and struggles. No matter what, we are going to keep doing what is right!

Things are slowly turning around for Jim and me. God is working everything out in His time according to His will. We included this chapter "From Then Until Now" to let you, the reader know what a difference God has made in our lives since we started writing this book in 2008 and until now May 2013. In the last two weeks, God has miraculously poured out His blessings on us. It started a few days ago when He provided us enough money to get our book "ONLY GOD" published, buy a 2002 Chrysler van, pay the back taxes owed on the house in South Fulton and Friendship, fix the hot water heater and dryer, buy food and other things we needed. We are now attending a church, where we can be used for God and His Kingdom. God has begun to open the door for our singing ministry, which we once thought had been put on the back burner. We believe it is only a matter of time before Jim gets a job that God wants him to have.

There is no limit to what God can do in our lives. God is able to do exceedingly abundantly above all that we ask or think, according to the power that works in us. (Ephesians 3:20)

In this world of hate and fear

Loneliness and despair are always near.

The only thing the world should see

Is the love of God abiding in me.

Chapter 19

Plan of Salvation

The Way To Jesus Christ Is Simple

Salvation is a very personal decision. This is something between you and God. The choice is yours alone.

1. Admit That You Are A Sinner

For all have sinned and come
short of the Glory of God

~Romans 3:23~

Admit to God you are a sinner. Sin is refusing to acknowledge God's authority over your life. Everyone sins. The result of sin is spiritual death or eternal separation from God when you die. Repent: turn away from your sin and toward God. (See Acts 3:19; Romans 3:23; 6:23).

2. Believe That Jesus Is The Son of God, Who Paid The Wages of Your Sin

For the wages of sin is death (eternal separation from God); but the gift of God is eternal life through Jesus Christ our Lord. ~Romans 6:23~

Believe in Jesus Christ as God's Son and accept Jesus' gift of forgiveness from sin. Jesus took the penalty for your sin by dying on the cross because you could not meet God's requirements for a perfect sacrifice for your sin. (See John 3:16).

3. Call Upon God.

If thou shalt confess with thy mouth to the Lord Jesus, and shall believe in thine heart that God hath raised Him from the head, thou shalt be saved.—Romans 10:9—Confess To God your faith in Jesus Christ as Savior and Lord. As Lord, Jesus has earned the right to be obeyed as a sheep obeys his shepherd. (See Romans 10:9-10, 13; I John 1:9).

Here is a little prayer you can say. Lord Jesus, I know You love me, because You died on the cross bearing my sins. Thank You, Jesus for revealing to me my lost condition. I ask you to forgive me of all sins that are in my life. I ask You Jesus to come into my heart. I am willing to change the direction of my life by acknowledging You as my Lord and Savior and by turning away from my sin. Thank You for giving me forgiveness, eternal life and hope in You, JESUS.

Don't Quit

When things go wrong, as they sometimes will,

When the road you're trudging seems all uphill,

When the funds are low, and the debts are high,

And you want to smile, but you have to sigh,

When care is pressing you down a bit,

Rest if you must, but don't you quit.

Life is queer with its twists and turns,

As every one of us sometimes learns,

And many a failure turns about,

When he might have won had he stuck it out;

Don't give us though the pace seems slow,

You may succeed with another blow.

Success is failure turned inside out,

The silver tint of the clouds of doubt,

And you never can tell how close you are,

It may be near when it seems so far.

So stick to the fight when you're hardest hit,

It's when things seem worse that you must not quit.

Author Unknown

God Can Move Your Mountain

When things seem so impossible

And life's so hard to bear,

God can move your mountain

Before you reach despair.

He will never leave you or forsake you-

Trust in Him always.

Be anxious then, for nothing

And never cease to pray.

So keep on climbing higher,

Be patient while you wait.

For God is never early

And He is never late.

~Author Unknown~

Jordan Heath Barber and Stacy Ann Puckett,
our son and daughter

I Asked God For.

I asked God to grant me patience.

God said, "NO!"

Patience is a by-product of tribulation.
It isn't granted. It is earned.

I asked God to give me happiness.

God said, "NO!"

I give you blessings. Happiness is up to you.

I asked God to spare me pain.

God said, "NO!"

Suffering draws you apart from worldly
cares and brings you close to me.

I asked God to make my spirit grow.

God said, "NO!"

You must grow on your own but I will
prune you to make you fruitful.

I asked for all things that I might enjoy life.

God said, "NO!"

I will give you life so that you may enjoy all things.

I asked God to help me love others,
as much as God loves me.

God said . . . "Ahhhh, finally you have the idea."

I Love You Always,

God

A Note From The Authors:

Jim and Carolyn Barber have dedicated their lives to God to be used by Him. Their heart's desire is to uplift Jesus before everyone and to help and encourage people.

They are founders of The Fathers Love Ministries, a non-profit organization. They also love to sing for Jesus. They call themselves The JNC Singers-Jim N Carolyn. They have a son, a daughter and 2 grandsons. They all make their home in South Fulton, TN.

To contact Jim N Carolyn:

Fathers Love Ministries
Jim N Carolyn Barber
8974 Brundige Rd.
South Fulton, TN. 38257

e-mail address:
jnc54@twc.com
fathers_love_ministries2013@yahoo.com

Website: http://bits-n-pieces-of-gold.weebly.com

Also look for Fathers LoveMinistries on Facebook